And (Anna) shepherded them
with integrity of heart.
With skillful hands
(s)he led them.

Psalm 78:72

" you can impress people
from a distance;
but you can only impact them
from up close. "
Howard Hendricks

Merry Christmas!
♡ Jaryn

What people are saying about …

TOP TEN WAYS TO BE A GREAT LEADER

"Most leadership books have a short shelf life, but Hans's book endures the test of time. This is a great read on servant leadership."

Dr. Rick Warren, founder of Saddleback Church
and author of *The Purpose Driven Life*

"Many equate leadership with knowledge or talent, but in today's workplace people don't necessarily follow knowledge or talent. Both are easy to find, and having them may actually be a deterrent to effective leadership. *Top Ten Ways to Be a Great Leader* shows us the characteristics that real leaders possess. And fortunately, they can be learned by anyone with a heart for true leadership."

Dan Miller, career coach, bestselling author,
and president of 48 Days LLC

"Whenever my friend Hans Finzel writes or speaks about leadership, he has my full attention. His insights are compelling because they are grounded in truth, tested by experience, and on full display in and through his life and ministry."

Dr. Crawford W. Loritts, Jr., author, speaker, radio host, and
senior pastor of Fellowship Bible Church, Roswell, GA

"*Whew!* Just when you think you can preach and teach Leadership 401, Hans Finzel writes another gem. He is so gifted at connecting the leadership dots. This is a jam-packed treasure chest of wisdom and fresh insights, oozing with the right blend of pokes in the ribs ... and grace."

John Pearson, author of *Mastering the Management Buckets* and board governance and management consultant at John Pearson Associates, Inc.

"Are you ready to ignite your leadership game to the next level? Then this book is a must read. Hans Finzel speaks from a huge reservoir of real life leadership experience when he maps out the ten essential skills that every effective leader must master. Whether you are just getting started or have decades of experience, I highly recommend the leadership wisdom that falls out of every page of this exciting new book."

John Lee Dumas, host of Entrepreneur On Fire and creator of The Freedom Journal and *The Mastery Journal*

"When Hans Finzel wrote his bestselling book, *The Top Ten Mistakes That Leaders Make*, I thought it was one of the greatest leadership books of all time. I have been greatly impacted by it over the years! His newest book, *Top Ten Ways to Be a Great Leader*, is destined to be a best seller because it is down-to-earth practical and is based on Hans's many years of leadership experience. I highly recommend it to anyone interested in becoming a great leader or anyone wanting to develop leaders who can make a difference in a world that is desperate for character-based leadership."

Stan Toler, bestselling author and speaker

"Hans's lessons on leadership and personal development always come from a place of principle. And principles are timeless. That's why his books and teaching will be part of my life today and for a long time into the future. I highly recommend this latest contribution to great leadership instruction."

Curt Beavers, international entrepreneur

"When it comes to leadership, you are either average or a warrior. I am thrilled about this latest leadership warrior-training book from Hans, *The Top Ten Ways to Be a Great Leader.* As a business owner, business consultant, business mentor, and entrepreneur, I know the real deal when I see it. We have too many leaders out there that are floundering and making things up as they go. I highly recommend this book for leaders on the ten essential skills all effective leaders must master."

Mike Agugliaro, business warrior of CEO Warrior

"I have found Hans Finzel's books on leadership refreshingly honest and immediately applicable in my multiple roles of Christian leadership. This one is no exception. If the delicate triad of knowledge, character, and skill woven throughout this book is maintained, it will extend one's time and effectiveness in leading God's work forward."

Mark L. Bailey, senior professor of Bible exposition
and president of Dallas Theological Seminary

"Look long enough and you will discover that everything rises or falls on leadership. Along with many popular simplistic approaches to leadership are the abstract theoretical approaches—big on theory but light on application. Hans Finzel has bridged these two extremes. In this delightful book, Hans allows theory to inform practice and then fleshes it out with real workplace examples. If you want to grow your leadership, these ten principles will help fuel your journey."

Mick Ukleja, PhD, president of LeadershipTraQ

"*Top Ten Ways to Be a Great Leader* reads like a series of personal mentoring conversations with Hans Finzel about critical leadership topics, overflowing from his more than three decades of experience. Within twenty-four hours of reading it, I found myself recounting insights from Hans to another leader facing a challenge addressed in this excellent book. Read it for yourself, then share his wisdom with others."

Steve Moore, president of nexleader

"Hans's honest approach and use of personal experiences help bring these key lessons home in a very authentic, clear, and practical way. If you are a leader who has been wanting to sit at the feet of someone a few steps down the road from you, or if you are simply wanting a checkup on how you are doing and how you can go further, then pick up this book and journey with Hans. You will not regret it."

Andrew Scott, president and CEO of Operation Mobilization USA

TOP TEN
WAYS TO BE
A GREAT
LEADER

TOP TEN
WAYS TO BE
A GREAT
LEADER

HANS FINZEL

David C Cook®
transforming lives together

TOP TEN WAYS TO BE A GREAT LEADER
Published by David C Cook
4050 Lee Vance Drive
Colorado Springs, CO 80918 U.S.A.

David C Cook U.K., Kingsway Communications
Eastbourne, East Sussex BN23 6NT, England

The graphic circle C logo is a registered trademark of David C Cook.

The website addresses recommended throughout this book are offered as a
resource to you. These websites are not intended in any way to be or imply an
endorsement on the part of David C Cook, nor do we vouch for their content.

Details in some stories have been changed to protect
the identities of the persons involved.

LCCN 2016959762
ISBN 978-0-7814-1462-3
eISBN 978-0-7814-1483-8

© 2017 Hans Finzel
Published in association with the literary agency of
Mark Sweeney & Associates, Naples, FL 34113.

The Team: Tim Peterson, Keith Jones, Amy Konyndyk,
Debbie Howell, Abby DeBenedittis, Susan Murdock
Cover Design: Nick Lee

Printed in the United States of America
First Edition 2017

1 2 3 4 5 6 7 8 9 10

011217

To Peter Pendell, my friend, mentor, and personal pastor. You have genuinely cared for my soul and spiritually nurtured me for decades. I appreciate your courage to speak honestly with me, man to man. Thank you for being the real deal as you walk the walk with Jesus. No wonder they call you the "pastor's pastor." I count it a privilege to be called your friend. Thank you for your investment in my leadership.

A friend loves at all times, and a brother is born for a time of adversity.
Proverbs 17:17

CONTENTS

FOREWORD

Hans Finzel has the broadest grasp of leadership of any person I have encountered. He relates leadership to the real world in such practical terms. I've had so much fun reading this, his newest book on leadership, because Hans is a truly brilliant communicator. If you enjoyed his *The Top Ten Mistakes Leaders Make*, you must read this companion book. That book was what to avoid. This is about what to master in leadership.

As a life coach and business strategist, I am consistently asked who mentors me in leadership. Hands down, my answer is Hans Finzel. Over the years, Hans's influence has made me the leader that I am, and I continue to follow his advice and use his insights. He looks at all aspects of leadership and is always adding the best to his toolbox. He then passes those tools on in a fun-to-follow way.

In his latest work, *Top Ten Ways to Be a Great Leader*, Hans gives razor-sharp information in a way that is easily applied. The philosophies, mind-sets, and action steps that he lays out in this book will make you a better leader, even a *great* leader.

I love that he addresses an area of leadership that most forget about. Tackling the areas of emotional intelligence and pride, Hans unpacks key aspects of why we don't listen. Everyone teaches us to listen, but Hans addresses the reasons why we don't.

What Hans has written on emotional intelligence blew me away! I told Hans, "You are the most effective communicator I have heard on this critical subject. Your teaching on emotional intelligence is better than any of the many top resources I have used to teach on the subject." I've already used these excellent key concepts in my own teaching.

What you have in your hands is practical, workable, and highly useful information for your own leadership. Just when I think I have a good grasp on leadership, Hans comes up with a new concept that brings me one of those "aha" moments that sharpen my skills even more.

I have had the privilege of working up close and personal with Hans and Donna Finzel. I believe the tools in this book are perfect for those in executive leadership. This is also a perfect Leadership 101 for the new entrepreneur just starting out and learning to be a leader for the first time.

Kathrine Lee
Founder of Pure Hope Foundation, life
coach, business strategist, and creator
of The Ultimate Source

INTRODUCTION

Whenever I speak to audiences on leadership, I ask this question: "How many of you have ever worked for a terrible boss?" Not only do 90 percent of the hands go up, but I also get all kinds of rolling eyes and groans. It's as if people are saying to me, "Oh wow, Hans, let me tell you about the jerk I had to work under."

When it's your turn to lead, what will others say about you? No leader is perfect, but I am assuming you picked up this book because your desire is to improve your leadership skills. Good for you. I think I can help. Here is my first piece of leadership advice: *don't do what comes naturally.* Trust me on this. Who are we really in our own human natures? I think most of us are naturally self-centered, looking out for ourselves first. Think about this. Do we have to teach young children to fight over toys? No. Not at all. They love to scream, "Mine!" The kind of leadership I advocate is the opposite: focusing on others first. Great leadership is not about *me.* It is about *we.* It is what I call *servant leadership*—caring more about the good of my team than my own enrichment.

Sure, we have some good gut-level instincts that will serve us well in leadership. But I have observed that there are more bad leaders out there than good ones; more incompetent managers than healthy ones. This is because so many of them are out first and foremost for their own careers and their own benefits. This is true in business, ministry, church, education, military, sales, and government.

Did you hear about Robert Rizzo, the incompetent city manager of Bell, California? He became a symbol of municipal greed and "was sentenced … to twelve years in prison—less than half the time it will take the nearly bankrupt Los Angeles suburb to dig itself out of the estimated $150 million in debt he left behind."[1] He and his cronies were living high on the hog with zero accountability, spending the city into ruin. Sometimes I look at someone in a position of leadership and just scratch my head and wonder, "How did he *ever* get appointed to that job?"

So why do I advise you not to start your leadership career by doing what comes naturally? Because of our natural tendency to look out for ourselves first. Serving others does not come naturally. We fall into mistakes and poor habits that perpetuate the terrible-boss epidemic. Face it: many of us have had a lot of poor role models in our working career. We repeat the poor mistakes we have seen in our awful bosses.

I have been leading and watching leaders for thirty years. Here are a few of my lifetime leadership axioms:

- If you do what comes naturally, you will be a poor leader.

- People are confused about how to be a great
  leader because of poor role models. In other
  words, we lead as we were led.
- There seem to be more bad leaders than good
  leaders.
- The world needs more great leaders.

My passion is to help produce more great leaders for all disciplines. I love mentoring leaders into a place of healthy influence where they empower those under them, not frustrate them. You don't want those you lead to be raising their hands in my audiences, do you?

Let me be clear about something from the get-go: I am not writing this book because I consider myself a great leader. No, it is born out of the many mistakes I have made and the wisdom I have learned over the years of practicing leadership. Although I have written a number of other books on leadership, I have never spelled out what I believe are the basic leadership "must-haves." The book you now hold in your hands is a great primer for those of you just entering into leadership. But it is also great for those of you who have experience in leadership but hunger to improve your game. This book will examine the essential skills and characteristics you must have to be an effective leader.

How would you respond if I asked you these questions: What are the most important skills you want your leaders to practice? What matters most to you about the personal character of your leaders? As I was writing this book, I asked my podcast listeners to answer this question: "What is one essential characteristic of a great leader whom you would respect and love to follow?" I also turned the question around and asked it this way: "What are the biggest blind spots you have seen in your leaders, which frustrate you big-time?" I wish I could hear your answers.

I combined the answers of my listeners with my own thirty years of leadership experience and pondered my own response. These ten chapters present the essential skills I believe every new leader must master. Using the letters in the word LEADERSHIP, I share my advice for both the hungry new leader and the seasoned leader looking for fresh help. At the end of each chapter, for those of you who want to dig deeper, I give you and your team some action points and discussion questions.

How would you define leadership? Is there one key to it? Are leaders born or are they made? Leadership is a complicated topic. It reminds me of trying to define *love*. So much has been written about both, and hundreds of definitions swirl around. After a lot of searching, I found the simple one-word definition for leadership I like best: *influence*. Every time you influence someone to take an action, positive or negative, you are leading that person. That applies in your home, your church, your community, your job, and your life.

> I found the simple one-word definition for leadership I like best: *influence*. Every time you influence someone to take an action, positive or negative, you are leading that person.

If you're in a position to influence others, keep working at your leadership skill set. If you have the gift of leadership, remember that Paul said in Romans we should work hard at sharpening it our whole lives: "If God has given you leadership ability, take the responsibility seriously" (Rom. 12:8 NLT).

"L" IS FOR LISTEN AND LEARN

My friend Chuck works for a global aerospace firm in Southern California. He told me a crazy story recently about when his "big boss" came to town to fix some problems and "listen to the troops." Chuck is in his early thirties and has to deal with some of the generational tension between his youthful team and baby boomer bosses. Chuck shared with me, "Our boss flew in from Saint Louis to have a big meeting with all of us on the team. He wanted to hear our concerns and learn what was causing problems in our production output. We spent all morning in a conference room with this gentleman, and—would you believe it?—every single issue we brought up he shot down with excuses. He blamed us and refused to listen to our concerns at all. It was like talking to a brick wall. He spent all morning rationalizing, making excuses, and belittling any legitimate concerns we brought up."

I asked Chuck, "So how did that make you feel?" He said he and his colleagues left that meeting extremely discouraged, with their tails between their legs. "We wondered why that big boss bothered to fly out to see us. He did not listen to one word we said. He made us feel terrible. It makes us all want to quit and find a better place to work."

I am always amazed to hear stories like this. Isn't it crazy how many people get into top management positions who have no business being there? I am sure you have scratched your head a time or two, wondering how an incompetent person ever got promoted to that place of leadership.

I love the topic of leadership because leaders make things happen. Leaders affect all of us, whether we lead, follow, or try to stay out of the way. History is the story of leaders, good and bad, who have done amazing good and terrible evil. I have a passion to help people starting out in leadership get on the right track and avoid the awful mistakes that make life miserable for followers.

Think about the question I told you I ask audiences when I start my talks on leadership: "How many of you have ever worked for a terrible boss?" When I ask that "terrible boss" question, it is as if 90 percent of the audience raising their hands are saying, "If only you knew the half of it!" When I drill down into the stories of these folks and their experiences, I am amazed at how often the issue of listening comes up—or really, the lack of listening. "Our team leader is so arrogant—she just does not listen. She is the world's expert on everything. I think she loves to hear herself talk!" I hear story after story of frustrated followers who wish they could be heard.

The problem of poor listening has increased dramatically in the last decade, particularly due to smartphones and the ubiquitous presence of the Internet and advertising. Now I even get attacked when I am filling up my car at the pump, with a little screen screaming advertisements at me. And social media addiction has taken distraction to a whole new level. Have you noticed that fewer people than ever really listen to you in the midst of all the disruption of technology? How do you feel when someone really does listen deeply to you? When we are really heard, we feel *valued*. I feel, in those rare moments, that my leader really does care about me.

If you are just starting out as a leader, this lesson is one of the most important you will hear from me. Hardly any behavior hurts followers more than a leader who does not know how to listen.

> Hardly any behavior hurts followers more than a leader who does not know how to listen.

TWO IDEAS JOINED AT THE HIP

The "L" in LEADERSHIP stands for two very important words: *listen* and *learn*. It has been my observation that one greatly affects the other. People who don't do well with one generally don't practice the other. If you are not willing to be a lifelong learner, why should you listen to great ideas from other people? Conversely, can you learn and grow without listening?

Great leaders know how to listen to their teams, and they are lifelong learners. People like to work with that kind of leader.

Listening and learning are vital, and I want to unpack each skill separately. If you just work on these two skills, you are going to set a great foundation for your future leadership.

LEARNING TO LISTEN

How good a listener would people around you say you are? I want you to think about your own listening skills. At the end of this chapter, I have an exercise for you that will help you find out how great or poor you are as a listener. For some people, listening comes naturally. But for many of us, it is a struggle. And even though we might be the leader, we're not the only ones with a voice; we have to learn to listen to our team.

I want you to feel what followers like Chuck feel when they have to suffer under leaders who don't listen. Here is my short list of the painful eight:

How do you feel if you are not listened to? I feel ...

1. Unimportant.
2. Marginalized.
3. It's a waste of time trying.
4. I am invisible.
5. My opinions are not respected.
6. I am not respected.
7. I have nothing to contribute.
8. Nothing is going to change.

I'm sure you can add to this list, but those points cover the most common reactions to leaders who don't listen. Many of these relate to the idea of respect. Lack of respect is a huge issue in the workplace. Followers can tell whether the leader respects them by how well she listens. Kohei Goshi, former chairman of the Japan Productivity Center, once said, "It may be difficult to teach a person to respect another unless we can help people to see things from the other's point of view."[1]

Here's what I've observed: *most leaders love to talk*. They enjoy listening to their own pearls of wisdom and great insights. "People should listen to me because I am the boss!" Sometimes they even begin to believe their own press. They only listen to positive feedback and things outsiders say about them. Outsiders who don't work with them might think they are awesome, but those on the inside know better! If your leaders have this unrealistic view of themselves, they claim more and more authority as they believe they have less and less reason to listen to subordinates. One of the curses of leadership is being isolated at the top of the pile, the king of the mountain.

Have you ever noticed that there's much more horizontal communication in an organization than vertical? Coworkers talk often with one another about all sorts of things, but the communication between those coworkers and their superiors is much less frequent and tends to be a lot more formal.

The book of James has great advice for all of us: "You must all be quick to listen, slow to speak, and slow to get angry"

(James 1:19 NLT). It's interesting—as I talk to so many followers and employees who feel stuck in miserable jobs, I often dig down into what it is about their boss that really frustrates them. It's amazing how often I hear the words, "Our boss just doesn't listen to us. It is always one-way communication." We should really all listen to the book of James.

I have been flying Southwest Airlines a lot lately. Southwest has a refreshing culture that is different from most airlines, some of which don't seem to care about their customers. The culture at Southwest was set by the founder, Herb Kelleher. He listened to his troops, and he was passionate about empowering people at the "bottom" of the company: flight attendants and gate agents. When you talk to a gate agent at Southwest, he actually listens to you. When you call Southwest's customer service, they really seem to care. They solve your problems without having to go up the chain of command for permission. Responding to the needs of the people you work with communicates that you really care about them.

The more people you lead, the more you have to listen, but the harder it becomes. Effective leadership has more to do with listening than with talking, because through listening—and we'll see this as you read on—you gain more wisdom and insight. If you listen to the people in the trenches and rely on their information, you will make better decisions. Chuck's boss lost a great opportunity to improve their company because he refused to accept constructive input. Sadly, he learned nothing new on that trip—he missed out on information that could have greatly helped their company.

A lot of leaders get stuck in isolation because they are at the top of a large organization and lose touch with the front lines. Whether it's people to whom you're ministering, people to whom you're providing a service, or people to whom you're selling things, you have to learn that the end user is king. It is for that person's sake that you do what you do. The higher you go in leadership, the more you're isolated and insulated from those people on the front lines. That's one of the biggest reasons you have to learn to listen to your people. Herb Kelleher never forgot this powerful principle, even when Southwest Airlines grew to be the largest domestic carrier of people in North America.

For twenty years, I served as CEO of a global nonprofit. I know what it is like to have too many demands from too many people. When we start out

> The higher you go in leadership, the more you're isolated and insulated from those people on the front lines.

in leadership, we might just have one or two people looking to us to lead them. But what if we are wildly successful? What if we get promoted? Or what if our team grows, and before we know it, we have dozens of people expecting us to be an example of a caring leader? What will happen if our team grows to an organization of hundreds? This is a great problem to have, but it brings its own problems with it!

Say you are successful and you have more and more people reporting to you. You get a big promotion. Your team is growing. Or say you just got a new job with direct reports for the first time.

Maybe your church or ministry is growing and you are hiring staff for the first time. As you embark on this journey of leading more and more people, you will face huge new challenges. The list that follows unpacks some leadership growing pains that make it hard to listen to everyone as your span of control grows.

WHY IT'S TOUGH FOR BUSY LEADERS TO LISTEN

Too little time. The more people you lead, the less time you have for each person. And, of course, the more demands each of them has of you. "Wow," you might think to yourself, "I used to have a lot more time for me before I got this team!" The telecommunications revolution is tightening the information noose around the neck of the average leader. Leaders can become so saturated with communication that they find their systems shutting down from a time-crunch overload.

Too many people. As I led our ministry, I needed to have a strong relationship with dozens of leaders in our organization, including the top leaders in the home office, the leaders of our field offices in North America, our international directors, and the sixty-plus leaders of our projects around the world. There were just too many of them to keep up with. But they could each get frustrated with me if I didn't take the time or build the systems whereby they could communicate with me. Most people in your organization want a piece of the leader at one time or another. And they want you to take the time to listen to them. And thus the *crisis* *of expectations*: the more people there are, the harder it is to link up with them and listen.

Too much pressure. Leaders find themselves under constant pressure from deadlines and responsibilities they can barely handle alone. You have the onslaught of email, texts, and social media. There are so many ways people can bombard us. The image of a soldier in battle comes to mind. Here I sit in the trenches. Bullets are flying everywhere, planes are buzzing overhead, tanks are rolling in my direction, and the radio is crackling with news from many fronts. In the midst of this, along comes one of my people who wants a long, quiet conversation about his concerns. The extreme pressure of leadership sometimes makes it very difficult to listen attentively. It seems like it's harder than ever to just stop and listen. Even as you're reading this book, I'll bet you're distracted. You're likely multitasking, not simply concentrating on my words. How many times have you stopped in this chapter to coddle your phone? If you managed to stay focused, congratulations. I know that's an accomplishment!

Too big a distance. In some cases, the problem of physical distance between the leader and her followers makes it tough to stay in close contact. My wife, Donna, leads a team of direct sales specialists who are physically located all over North America. She spends a *lot* of time connecting with her team via phone, Skype, Zoom, Voxer, and other applications. At times she gets frustrated because she cannot simply sit down with them and have a face-to-face conversation. In my leadership ministry, I had the added challenge of many of our top leaders living thousands of miles away from me, some of them on other continents.

Too much knowledge. Leaders sometimes know so much that they find it hard to listen to people rehearsing stories, facts, or anecdotes they have already heard a thousand times. As your team member is droning on, you are thinking, "Okay, I have already heard that story," or, "Tell me something I don't know!" The more knowledge we have and the more we've experienced, the harder it is to listen to others patiently. I am often tempted to say, "Give me the *Reader's Digest* version!" Pride may also be involved, coming on the heels of the knowledge problem. Sometimes we think we know too much; we get to the place where we don't think we can learn from others. That's why I'll devote the final chapter of this book to the problem of pride and the power of humility in leadership.

Nothing stops the progress of an organization more quickly than leaders failing to listen. Followers want to communicate with their leaders. If you fail to listen to them, their very effectiveness and job satisfaction will be in jeopardy. You don't have to agree with them, but they need to know they were heard.

> Nothing stops the progress of an organization more quickly than leaders failing to listen.

I've had people say to me, "Hans, I just don't feel you're a good listener." I hate it when somebody says that to me. I take it personally because I try to be a good listener. If I dig into what's really behind that statement, it is often the fact that I didn't do what they wanted me to do. That's the price of leadership. We have to make hard decisions, and leadership is not a popularity contest. So sometimes people say "You don't listen" just because you ignore their advice. That's different from not being a good listener. A good leader will let people sense they have been heard, even if their advice is not followed. At the end of this chapter I share some action points about how to practice the feedback loop.

FOUR FACTORS OF DOUBT

One reason people might say you don't listen well is that you shut down doubt. Do you get defensive when people disagree with you? I learned this lesson when we were moving our offices from Chicago to Denver. We left a terribly broken building in Wheaton, Illinois, and built a brand-new, fifty-thousand-square-foot international headquarters in Littleton, Colorado. The decision affected a lot of our employees and their families. Even though we as leaders (the senior staff and board of directors) thought it was a great idea, we had many detractors who were skeptical when we announced the decision. Some thought it was a stupid idea, and others thought we were going to destroy our organization.

I eventually realized through that journey that shutting down the doubters was counterproductive. I learned that what Spencer Johnson said in *Who Moved My Cheese?* is very true: "A change imposed is a change opposed."[2] We as leaders need to *embrace doubt*—not shut it down. That's when I came up with this list of the four factors of doubt. When changes are imposed on people, it is human nature for them to push back. As the leader, my job is to address the doubt every step of the way down this spiral.

1. It ain't broke. "We did not know there was a problem!" That's the first reaction when changes are announced. This is when people first begin doubting. All of a sudden, they are being asked to move from A to B, and they love A. Our first job as leaders of change is to show them why A is broken and why we need to move to B. For my team, many members loved living in Chicago and did not realize our building was so very broken.

2. Don't fix it. "We're in shock about your solution to a non-problem." That's the "don't fix it" issue; don't fix what's not broken. You as the leader might be totally convinced that a change is necessary, but that does not mean your team sees what you see. In our situation, we had to build a case for change and show our team why we had to get a new facility and why moving to Colorado made economic and strategic sense.

3. We are being ambushed. "We had no idea change was coming. We felt ambushed." This is when the leader just steps up and says to the team, "It has been decided." Their first question is, of course, "Who decided?" And the second question follows naturally upon the first: "Why were we not involved?" Sometimes decisions have to be made behind closed doors, like our relocation. In those cases, it is much harder to get buy-in from followers. I have a friend who likes to say, "If they are not up on it, they are down on it."

4. We gave no input. This is when the followers say, "We offered no input for the solutions imposed on us. We might have actually had a better solution." And guess what? They usually do have good input that you can use. Wherever possible, be very open about change ideas. Run them past your team *before* you implement new things.

After the move to Colorado, it took me a few years to recover from some of the misunderstandings that had occurred because I was a young, green leader. I learned to embrace doubt, not shut it down. Being a good listener takes a lot more time than being a dictator. But you get much better results.

So what happens if you are a good listener? Well, I'll turn the list I gave you earlier in the chapter around. How would Chuck and his

> Being a good listener takes a lot more time than being a dictator. But you get much better results.

team have felt if the big shot from Saint Louis had taken the time to hear them without being defensive? How will your followers feel if you're a good listener and you take the time to listen to their concerns?

How do you feel if you are listened to? I feel …

1. I am important—instead of unimportant.
2. I am an essential part of the team—instead of marginalized.
3. I matter to my boss—instead of a waste of time trying.
4. I am visible!—instead of invisible.
5. My voice is respected—instead of my opinions are not respected.

6. I am respected—instead of I am not respected.
7. I matter—instead of I have nothing to contribute.
8. Real change is coming—instead of nothing is going to change.

LIFELONG LEARNING

> "The most notable trait of great leaders, certainly of great change leaders, however, is their quest for learning. They show an exceptional willingness to push themselves out of their own comfort zones, even after they have achieved a great deal."
>
> —Frances Hesselbein and Paul Cohen, *Leader to Leader*[3]

The second key word that comes to mind for the "L" in LEADERSHIP is *learn*. It is the flip side of the "L" coin. And while I am adding words that start with the letter "L," you'll see I also slipped in *lifelong*. If we stop learning today, we will stop leading tomorrow. This never changes. We never arrive at a place of full knowledge about our work. And we certainly never arrive at a place of maturity. One of the most mature leaders in the New Testament was the apostle Paul. After decades of leadership experience, he said,

Not that I have already obtained all this, or have already arrived at my goal, but I press on to take

hold of that for which Christ Jesus took hold of
me. Brothers and sisters, I do not consider myself
yet to have taken hold of it [*arrived, mature*]. But
one thing I do: Forgetting what is behind and
straining toward what is ahead, I press on toward
the goal to win the prize for which God has called
me heavenward in Christ Jesus. (Phil. 3:12–14)

Paul was saying that he had not yet matured and become
perfect. He was on a lifelong journey of becoming all that God
wanted him to be. We all have to be lifelong learners. We are living
in a day of such rapid change that our college degree is obsolete
soon after commencement. Whatever training you might have,
formal or informal, it is a great foundation for what you are doing
now—but it's not enough.

How can you learn new things and become even more hungry
to grow as a person? Step one is to be an open vessel. French scien-
tist Claude Bernard said it so well: "It is what we think we know
already that often prevents us from learning." The hunger to grow
and learn is the opposite of pride.

I was talking to Donna about this chapter, and she said,
"Be sure to mention how important it is to invest in your own
development." Self-improvement is critical to growing in your
leadership. Thank you, Donna, for that great advice, because
it's so true. She's been in her business for fifteen years, and I
watch her improve and the people she's working with improve as
they grow. Everyone who succeeds in her line of work becomes a

leader. They all build teams that create a huge need for personal growth, and often they are stepping into a role of leading others for the first time. If they want to become more successful, they have to pay attention to their own personal development. My good friend David Beavers, who works in the same company Donna is in, says that "our business is a personal development program cleverly disguised as a business."

I have a sign on my desk that reads, "Life begins at the end of your comfort zone." It reminds me to grow every day and keep learning new things that sometimes scare me. Reading this book is a great example of striving to improve your leadership. Going to seminars, reading great books, listening to podcasts, and getting feedback are all constructive.

HOW A GREAT LEADER LEARNED TO GROW

I enjoy studying great leaders in the Bible. One of my favorites is Moses. I wrote a book about his leadership, *The Top Ten Leadership Commandments*. I love Moses because he was a reluctant leader who succeeded at leading a tough group of people across a desert for forty years without giving up. Talk about a tough leadership calling! But Moses was a lifelong learner. As important as he was, as powerful as he was, as much responsibility as he had, he still listened and learned.

In Genesis, there's a classic story about Moses and his father-in-law, Jethro. I call Jethro the first management consultant in the Bible. Right after a huge leadership success, Moses had to learn an important lesson. The message came through his father-in-law. Who might be trying to give you messages that you need to hear about improving your leadership? Are you willing to listen to their voices?

Moses bragged to Jethro about all the amazing things that had happened through his leadership—taking the children of Israel through the Dead Sea and then watching their enemies drown before their eyes. The Bible doesn't say whether Moses took the time to play with his children or spend time with his wife or work on his marriage and his family; there's nothing in there about that. We are left to our own imaginations. We do know that Moses sent his wife and his kids away to live with the in-laws because he was so busy doing the work of God. His father-in-law sent him a message: "Moses, I'm coming back to see you and, by the way, I'm bringing your family with me" (see Exod. 18:6).

When Jethro arrived on the scene, he was delighted to hear about all the good things Moses had done for Israel and how he and God as a team rescued God's people from the hands of the Egyptians. That night, Jethro went to bed and pondered Moses's situation. He loved and respected his son-in-law and wanted to give him some important advice.

The next day, Jethro truly got the picture of why Moses was so busy—too busy for his family. All day long, people lined up to get advice from him. The line was out the doorway of the tent and around the block. When his father-in-law saw all that

Moses was doing, he said, "What is this you are doing for the people? Why do you alone sit as judge, while all these people stand around you from morning till evening?" (v. 14). Can you imagine? People stood around all day waiting for Moses to solve their problems. That's a leader with a problem. Jethro looked at Moses and said, "What you are doing is *not good*" (v. 17).

The advice from Jethro to Moses was clear. It is great advice for all of us. He told Moses to build a team and learn to delegate (vv. 21–23). He would lighten his load by sharing it with others. Jethro basically said, "You need to appoint other people to help you. You don't have to be a control freak; you alone don't have to do everything. You have to spread the load, you have to build a team, you have to be able to spend time with your family. You have to have time off. You're going to burn yourself out."

Can you imagine how stressed-out Moses was and how frustrated all these people were as they waited in line to see him? They would be happy to talk to somebody else to get their conflicts resolved or their problems answered. Jethro helped Moses learn to be team-centered in his leadership. The coolest thing is "Moses listened to his father-in-law and did everything he said" (v. 24). Unlike many leaders, Moses actually learned and changed his leadership habits.

I've seen too many leaders fail in their professional lives for personal reasons. It often had to do with this kind of workaholic lack of balance. But not only did Moses back off from his work and appoint other leaders to help him, he reengaged with his wife and kids. Jethro gave Moses's wife and kids back to him:

"Here you go. These are your responsibilities. I'm out of here. I love my grandkids, but you need to raise them."

There's not a single one of us who doesn't have areas in which we need to grow. Remember the "L" in LEADERSHIP, the first of the ten critical characteristics every new leader must master: be a good *listener* and a *lifelong learner*.

ACTION POINTS AND DISCUSSION QUESTIONS

Here are some action points that will help you grow in your ability to listen and learn as a new leader. And you can turn each of these into discussion questions for a group study with your team.

1. Sharpen your listening skills with feedback. If you really want to sharpen your listening skills, ask the people you work with, "Hey, how would you rate me as a listener on a scale of one to ten?" And once they give you the number, ask: "Please tell me why you gave me that score. And tell me how I can do a better job of listening." When they tell you, please don't be defensive. You might need to ask the question behind the question, but they will tell you how you come across.

2. Try feeding back to people what they said to you. This is a great listening skill because, remember, communication is not a one-way street. It is not just giving out information—it is getting through. Test to see if what you are hearing is really what they are saying. The best way to be sure is to say, "Okay, let me tell you what I just heard you say," and then simply say it back to them. They can either agree or correct your understanding. And if you go out and do something different, at least they know they were heard. Try some role-play with this as a team.

3. There is no substitute for face time with your team. I was using that term long before Apple installed FaceTime on their devices. Sometimes you really have to have personal, one-on-one face time with your people. As much as I love technology, there are times when we really need to sit down with people. A friend of mine who is a consultant was just fired by a client this morning. He asked me what I think happened—I was the one who got him the gig. I said, "I really think the client did not know you as a person. You spent no time alone building the relationship. It was all business, and the only time you saw the client was in meetings." My friend's client misunderstood and lacked trust in him because their relationship was never solidified over some good old-fashioned face time. Be sensitive to times when you need to have a direct face-to-face conversation with a member of your team.

4. Consume a regular diet of resources that help you grow. Read great books and articles, and listen to CDs and podcasts. Constantly sharpen your leadership game. I was telling somebody today that doctors, nurses, and all sorts of medical practitioners have to go to continuing medical education throughout their careers. They can't just graduate and say they're done—they have to keep their skills sharp for the rest of their lives. The same thing applies to leadership. A great way to get the most out of this book is to read it as a team. Meet for breakfast or lunch and discuss the action points at the end of each chapter.

"E" IS FOR EMOTIONAL INTELLIGENCE

Susan and Bev have been working together for several years. They work in a fantastic office environment, and they have a great working relationship ... except for a sore point in how they communicate. Susan is quite smart, but has one glaring blind spot that drives people crazy: she rocks in IQ but suffers in EQ.

This recent exchange exemplifies what has bugged Bev for all the years of their relationship. Can you see what is wrong with this picture?

Susan: "Hi, Bev, how was your weekend?"

Bev: "Dave and I drove our son Ben up to college in Pasadena and settled him into his dorm. It was tough seeing our last child go off to college. I cried a lot on the way home."

Susan: "I know. Bob and I had such a struggle when we took Courtney off to college five years ago. We did so much shopping getting everything ready for her. Even the dog was sad. Our road trip was fun but sad because we were taking her so far away, and it really was bittersweet. It was kind of hard to say good-bye, and then we blah, blah, blah, blah, blah …"

The conversation, as usual, seemed to be a one-way street. Susan never responded to Bev's opening volley of hurting emotions. Nope, not a single follow-up question. The spotlight always lands on Susan and stays there.

As smart and successful as Susan is, this blind spot makes people not want to talk to her. She is always talking about herself and her world. Ask anyone who knows her—she is highly competent but one-sided in conversations. This is the kind of person who is thinking about her comeback while you are talking, not really absorbing what you are saying. As soon as you are quiet, she interrupts with her own viewpoint, the cascade of words flowing out. She excels in sharing her own experience and opinion on everything related to the topic but does not value what *you* were trying to share with her.

Do you have people like that in your world? The two big issues that hurt Susan's leadership when it comes to working with others are that she talks too much and she never really listens. It is one-upmanship at its worst. I think, deep down, it is insecurity. She is trying too hard to be accepted, and it backfires.

WHAT IS EMOTIONAL INTELLIGENCE?

In chapter one, we talked about how hard it is to work with leaders who don't listen. In this chapter, we are going behind the curtain to unpack what might be at the root of those "listening and learning" problems.

The "E" in LEADERSHIP stands for *emotional intelligence*, also known as EQ—as opposed to IQ, which is our intelligence quotient. Success in leadership has so much more to do with EQ than with IQ. Through some of my own failures, I've come to believe that emotional intelligence is essential for effective, healthy leadership. The key word there is "healthy."

I want to give you a quick tour of the field of EQ. Perhaps this is all new to you—I only discovered

> Emotional intelligence is essential for effective, healthy leadership.

it myself in the last five years. After I give you an overview of what this is and why it is so important to you, I'm going to leave you with four action points you can use to apply what you've learned. I'm also going to tell you about a very cool EQ test you can take for free online.

As I was writing this chapter, I heard from my friend Chris in Germany who listens to my podcast on leadership (www.hansfinzel.com). I asked listeners to tell me what they think are the most essential skills every new leader must master. Chris wrote, "A new leader must know who they are, AND who they aren't. *They must understand themselves in order to lead others. Without this, the new leader will make the same mistakes over and over again.*"[1]

Thank you, Chris—excellent point. And that's how vital emotional intelligence is. It is about truly understanding how you come across to others as you try to lead them.

In response to the same question, a listener named Joe stated his conviction that "conscientiousness is the skill every budding leader must master before being able to lead effectively." Joe continued with the true application of conscientiousness and what he really meant by that big word: "The ability to *know one's self, as well as what others are perceiving about us,* is paramount to understanding if and when to move forward with a proposed plan or how to go about engaging with the varying personalities that compose a team."[2] I could not have expressed it better. This is exactly what emotional intelligence is all about. Both of these comments from my listeners speak to the nature of EQ.

We've always used IQ as the standard of how smart a person is.[3] Teachers and parents and the world around you make a big deal about IQ. And, by deduction, people think that the higher your IQ, the further you're going to go in life and the more effective you'll be in your career. I totally disagree with that premise. We all know smart people who are complete failures. One of my deep convictions about leadership, after practicing it, studying it, and watching effective leaders for over thirty years, is that IQ does not amount to much. Honestly, you know as well as I do that a lot of very smart people are abrasive jerks. It is EQ that has the biggest impact on long-term effectiveness in a job—and in success as a leader. If you are just starting out leading others, focus on growing in your people skills.

This leads me to feedback I received from Jordan in Illinois. She wrote this about my podcast: "It's not really just about leadership; it's about being a healthy person."[4] I love that. Yes, if you rank high in emotional intelligence, that means you project the aura of a healthy person. And as a healthy person, you are also an effective leader as more and more people follow you.

> It is EQ that has the biggest impact on long-term effectiveness in a job—and in success as a leader.

People don't like to follow dysfunctional leaders. They sometimes have to, but they don't want to. I've collected a lot of horror stories over the years about bad employers, team leaders, and bosses. Isn't it amazing how many dysfunctional people can become a boss or team leader? How do they get there when they are so unhealthy? It could be money, politics, or just the accidental fact that they got there first. What *you* need to focus on is becoming a healthy leader as you grow in your influence.

Traditionally, when evaluating someone for a job, managers tended to look for hard skills such as experience, degrees, training, and proficiency with a task. But according to recent research, performance success in leadership is one-third IQ and two-thirds EQ.[5] To put it another way, EQ counts for twice as much as IQ and technical skills combined if you want to be successful at leading others.

Emotional intelligence is about the soft skills of work and leadership, things like connecting with people by looking them in the eye when you're speaking to them, or walking into a crowded room and interacting with others rather than shying away into a corner. Of course, some of us are extroverts who naturally go into the crowd (like my wife, Donna), and some are introverts like me, who naturally look for the quiet corner. A healthy person has to be able to engage with people. As much as I love the quiet corner, I have learned to go into the crowd because it is part of working well with others.

WHAT ARE THE BUILDING BLOCKS OF EQ?

Do you want to grow in your EQ? Do you have the courage, and are you up to facing your flaws? John Ortberg says we need "Truth-Tellers" in our lives:

> Every one of us needs a few people to tell us the truth about our hearts and souls. We all have weak spots and blind spots that we cannot navigate on our own. We need someone to remind us of our deepest aspirations and values; we need someone to warn us when we may be getting off track. We need someone to help us question our motives

and examine our consciences. We need someone to perform spiritual surgery on us when our hearts get hard and our vision gets dim. We need a few Truth-Tellers.[6]

I am grateful to my good friend Dr. Mick Ukleja, who has pioneered some great work on EQ. I asked him to break down the areas of EQ so we can understand what we are really talking about. Ukleja says emotional intelligence is made up of five skill sets.[7] I have expanded on his list of five with my own brief explanations.

1. *Self-perception*—Do I really know my strengths and weaknesses?

2. *Self-expression*—How am I relating to others as a communicator? Do other people get what I am trying to say to them? Am I clear as I communicate?

3. *Interpersonal*—How well do I get along with the people I work with? Do I have good people skills?

4. *Decision making*—Do I make decisions for the good of the team? Do I make decisions in a timely manner, or do I linger too long keeping things open?

5. *Stress management*—How do I act when I am under a lot of pressure? Is what comes out a bad version of me that is off-putting?

I confess, during my years as a CEO I was not in touch with my EQ as I should have been, and that led me into some rough waters. I have three degrees, including a doctorate, but that is mostly head knowledge. As a leader, I struggled in the area of personal relationships with my team. It had a lot to do with my personality. In the next chapter, I'm going to get vulnerable about some of the issues I had. But I realize now how important it is for all of us leaders to get feedback from peers to identify our blind spots. That's the road toward good emotional intelligence.

Let me illustrate what I am talking about by telling you about two real-life people who worked for me (names have been changed throughout this book). Mary was amazing. She was naturally gifted and smart, and was very good at what she did. She knew her skill set well and performed her technical job with excellence. Everybody admired her skills in her arena. However, on the soft side of things, she became more and more difficult to work with. I can't tell you how many times people said, "You know, Hans, I feel like I'm walking on eggshells around her," or "I have to be so careful what I say because I don't know when she's going to explode." When upset, she was given to emotional blastoffs that made people very uncomfortable.

So what did we do about the problem of Mary? We did *not* just talk behind her back about how bad the situation was. We did *not* just grin and bear it. No, we confronted her, we tried to help her, we coached her,

> We confronted her, we tried to help her, we coached her, and we practiced patience with her. But eventually, we had to let her go.

and we practiced patience with her. But eventually, we had to let her go. It was so hard, because we had to part ways with a highly competent person who was doing great work for us. But people refused to work with Mary, so it was the soft side that did her in, not the hard side. The hard side was excellent and competent, but the soft side became unbearable, and it hurt the entire team. Sadly, Mary never understood why she was asked to leave our team. Her blind spot was untouchable.

Then there was Tony. It's a somewhat similar story. He was competent in his job, but he was hurting the organization with the way he treated people. He belittled others and made harsh offhand comments to them. He treated people like they were kindergartners and he was the principal. His lack of respect for coworkers was his undoing. Letting Tony go was one of the most difficult firings I ever had to face. I asked my board of directors for advice about him. They were emphatic: "You've tried, but it's not working. He is harming your leadership and the team too much. You have got to let him go—now." And I responded, "But can't we give him another chance?" I actually gave Tony another six months, and we did everything we could to coach him, but in the end, well, the board was right. Waiting another six months was not a good idea and made a very bad situation worse.

I know a lot of you struggle as I do with letting people go. Some of you work with volunteers you cannot fire. And some of you work in the kind of business where you get stuck with the people on your team and have to keep them. In a case like that, don't let them suck you dry. Ignore them, corral them if you can, and pour your focus on the people who fuel you and show the most promise for success.

I'm consulting with a leader right now who told me yesterday that he's finally letting someone go whom I told him a year ago he needed to release. Like many people in the ministry world, he kept giving this person one chance after another, thinking, *Perhaps he will magically get a new personality!* Not going to happen. Finally, he's biting the bullet. For those in ministry, it's hard to let people go, because we're all about love and compassion and forgiveness and grace. We want to give people the third chance, the fourth chance, the fifth chance. This makes it very difficult for us to have that horrible, painful conversation. I remember the day I let Tony go. It was a Friday afternoon, and he was going to have to go home to his wife and tell her he lost his job. It hurt me to the core to have to do that, but it was the right decision. Tony, like Mary, lost his ability to contribute to our team for lack of emotional intelligence.

> Emotional intelligence is the "something" in each of us that is a bit intangible. It affects how we manage behavior, navigate social complexities, and make personal decisions that achieve positive results. Emotional intelligence is made up of four core skills that pair up under two primary competencies: *personal competence* and *social competence.*
>
> —TalentSmart[8]

AN EQ BATTLE PLAN

I chose EQ as one of the top ten essential skills every new leader must master because it is so critical to your success. It is too important to leave out of a basic training book on leadership.

Assuming I have convinced you that you need to be an emotionally intelligent person, what do you do about it? How do you grow yourself and help your team grow in this? Is it even possible to create a healthy team when certain of our teammates are hurting for emotional intelligence? Let me give you four pointers related to driving your team, and yourself as well, toward emotional intelligence.

1. Talk to your team about EQ and study it together. You might want to read one of the books I list later in this chapter with your team. The topic of blind spots is a good place to begin. A safe way to start this conversation is to make an example of yourself and ask your teammates to join you in this. We know that people can raise their IQs to some degree, but Dr. Mick Ukleja has demonstrated that people can indeed raise their EQs too. It's possible to improve EQ and experience lasting gains that have a profound positive impact on lives as well as careers.

2. Perform team evaluations. Be careful with this, but seek and solicit feedback. Just as Joe said earlier in this chapter, you have to discover your blind spots from your peers. Be very careful that this process remains caring and respectful. People have to be committed to each other, and I think people have to be committed to the fact that this is an improvement process. It's meant to be restorative and constructive—not punitive. I've seen people use team performance evaluations and 360-degree evaluations as weapons, especially against bosses they're trying to get back at. Make sure your team doesn't do that. But you do need peer feedback to learn about your blind spots and help others with theirs. Go online and search for "team evaluations" or "360 reviews," and you will find a wealth of great tools to use.

3. Exercise confrontation and a developmental plan. A developmental plan is when you sit down with someone and give them that peer-review feedback: "Here's this blind spot—what are you going to do to grow and learn?" A leader I know described how his team identified a blind spot in his leadership practices. He said, "My problem was that I'd go into a meeting, and I was the boss. At the start of the meeting, I'd tell them all the conclusions regarding decisions we had to make that day, and then we started the meeting. I realized after getting feedback from the team that it made the meeting worthless because—who's going to disagree with the boss? They said, 'Look, instead of you coming into the meeting with your preconceived conclusions about everything, which means you don't value our input, why don't you start by giving us the agenda and then letting us discuss it? Why don't you listen, and at the end we will make these decisions? Otherwise, quit wasting our time with these meetings.'"

> Be honest with people about their blind spots and introduce a developmental plan.

And the leader really changed. That's what I'm talking about: learning about a blind spot and then changing. Be honest with people about their blind spots and introduce a developmental plan.

4. Part ways and release people if there is not major improvement. There are times when you just have to cut the ties. If you have a board, listen to their advice, as I failed to do with mine. I tried a developmental plan with both Mary and Tony, but in both cases, we had to let them go. Sometimes we have to part ways with people who are dragging down the ship. Mary could not manage stress. In Tony's case, it was a breakdown of interpersonal dimension, his ability to relate to other people. If you work with volunteers or people you cannot release, neglect them and pour yourself into the good people who show the most promise.

EQ RESOURCES

My friend Dr. Henry Deneen completed his doctoral dissertation on emotional intelligence. What I love about his work on this project is that he applied what he learned to his leadership team while he was a CEO. He made himself vulnerable to his team as he learned about his own blind spots. I interviewed him on one of my podcasts. Here is what he had to say about how important EQ is:

> In determining fitness for hiring or incompetency once hired, many employers focus on the

so-called *hard skills*, including indicators such as aggressiveness, follow-through, speed, being fast and persistent. While these are important issues in hiring, training, and equipping employees, they are by no means the only or even the most important factors. Incorporation of so-called *soft skills* may be of equal importance in determining the types of people to seek to represent an organization. These skills are defined as creativity, listening skills, team skills, being open to criticism, and being team players as well as areas of "personal competence" ... and "social competence" ... [that] constitute an individual's emotional intelligence.[9]

I think you get the idea that I believe EQ is a big deal for you as a new leader. In the decades to come, teams, companies, and ministries will focus on soft skills such as EQ as the way to succeed. Those who do will have the upper hand in whatever they are pursuing. Here are the six books I think are the best sources out there on EQ:

1. *Leadership and Self-Deception: Getting Out of the Box* by the Arbinger Institute
2. *Emotional Intelligence 2.0* by Travis Bradberry and Jean Greaves

3. *Awareness: The Perils and Opportunities of Reality* by Anthony De Mello

4. *Primal Leadership: Unleashing the Power of Emotional Intelligence* by Daniel Goleman, Richard Boyatzis, and Annie McKee

5. *Immunity to Change: How to Overcome it and Unlock the Potential in Yourself and Your Organization* by Robert Kegan and Lisa Laskow Lahey

6. *The Power of Full Engagement: Managing Energy, Not Time, Is the Key to High Performance and Personal Renewal* by Jim Loehr and Tony Schwartz

I would encourage you to consider acquiring these books if you wish to delve deeper into this topic.

ACTION POINTS AND DISCUSSION QUESTIONS

Your team would benefit from digging into the EQ of each of your members. Here are four action points and discussion questions that you and your team can implement and discuss:

1. Take the free EQ quiz at LeadershipTraq.com. See how you do, and think about what you can do to score higher in EQ. As a team, compare notes and see how much you can learn about one another. While you are talking as a team about blind spots, be sure to focus on positive traits too. This should not be one giant downer!

2. Read a good book on emotional intelligence. Check out the six I listed in this chapter. As a team, read one of these books together and meet monthly over breakfast or lunch to discuss what you are learning.

3. Perform some simple evaluations of your own emotional intelligence and your team's. Since emotional intelligence includes reality testing, it would be helpful to seek validation from your peers, coworkers, friends, and even family members. How do others perceive you? Feedback from others is essential for personal growth. I know it's a dangerous zone. In the next chapter, the "A" in LEADERSHIP stands for *accessibility*. I'll talk about how to be approachable and some of the pitfalls involved. If you make peer feedback mandatory, nobody gets singled out. Everybody goes through the same process with the same questions and the same steps. If you want to go really deep with your team, consider the instrument Henry Deneen used with his team, the Mayer-Salovey-Caruso Emotional Intelligence Test (MSCEIT), an ability-based test designed to measure four branches of emotional intelligence.

4. Listen to my podcast interviews with experts on emotional intelligence. On www.HansFinzel.com, listen to podcast episodes thirty-one and forty-two with Henry Deneen, who did his doctoral dissertation on emotional intelligence at Denver Seminary. Then listen to podcast episode sixty-two with my lifelong friend Mick Ukleja. A great group exercise would be to listen to and discuss these podcasts as a team.

3

"A" IS FOR ACCESSIBILITY

This week I talked to a very frustrated woman who is in leadership in her church. I'll bet you can relate to her anxiety. Naomi complained about people who always demand immediate responses to text messages and email. With great stress on her face, she asked, "Hans, is servant leadership dropping whatever I am doing to answer them immediately? They don't know anything about boundaries! Why can't people understand that they don't own me? I have a lot on my plate!"

This brings up a great balancing act for all leaders. How do I get the things done that are expected of me and still remain accessible to my team? I wish I had a super simple formula for success in this tension, but I don't. However, I do have the advice I gave to Naomi, which I will give to you in this chapter. Our people *are* our work, but we have to learn to balance their demands.

The "A" in LEADERSHIP stands for *accessibility*. Did you know that accessibility is absolutely essential for today's leaders? Gone are corner offices and executive floors. People, especially the younger generations, demand to have access to their team leaders. Along with accessibility, there is a partner word that is just as crucial today: *vulnerability*. One of the biggest mistakes you can make as a new leader is isolation and insulation from your team. If you are used to working alone, it can be a huge adjustment for you when, all of a sudden, other people are looking to you for leadership and invading your space. Worse yet, they might be asking you personal, probing questions that make you feel uncomfortable.

You might be a leader just starting out, or a seasoned one like Naomi. The accessibility principle applies to all of us who lead others. Do you lead people younger than you or older? Did you know that generations have a lot to do with how people want to communicate with each other? As an example, one of the younger women Donna relates to in her business only communicates via Facebook messages. That is really the only way to reach Susie. Then there is her older team member Harold, part of the builder generation, who just loves the telephone and email. Have you heard the saying that only old people use email? There is some truth to that. Boomers seem to love email, since it was invented by and for them.

I have seen older people react very negatively when younger people demand instant access. Some boomers and builders see this as an insulting, disrespectful, in-your-face approach to communication. But that is not what is going on. It is just a different expectation of accessibility—one with no barriers. The younger you are, the more at home you feel with many different ways of communicating. The social media revolution, high-speed Internet,

> The social media revolution, high-speed Internet, and smartphones have created an always-on, instant culture among many of the people you are going to lead.

and smartphones have created an always-on, instant culture among many of the people you are going to lead. Get used to it!

ARE YOU TASK-ORIENTED?

Task-oriented people struggle the most with being accessible to their teams. I know because I am one. I am your classic type A, task-oriented achiever. That is probably why I fell into leadership—I know how to get things done. Can you relate? The opposite kind of person is people-oriented. I have devised a simple test to determine whether you are task- or people-oriented. When you are working at your workspace and someone interrupts you, do you stop what you are doing, relax, smile, and engage with this person until the conversation comes to its natural conclusion? Or do you grimace inside and do anything you can to get the conversation done as quickly as possible so you can get back to your work? If your answer is the latter, then you are one of us: the type A personality who tends to measure success by getting his list checked off.

If someone calls you or messages you and says she needs to talk right away, how do you respond in your gut? "Great. What does she want now? I don't have time for this!" Or do you take the team leadership view: "I need to be there for her, and if she needs me this badly, I need to see what I can do to help." If it needs to be a longer conversation, we can schedule the right time to talk.

I know people who have it a lot worse than we do when it comes to unreasonable demands on our time. I've had opportunities to travel to many cultures of the world that are very different from ours in North America. The last time I was in Mali, I had the chance to spend a few days with my colleagues Nathan and Becky. They live with their three little children in a town of twenty thousand people with no electricity. They moved there from the United States to help the community with solar projects and job creation. Would you believe that, from sunup till after dark, the people of the village line up at their gate seeking help? Some want money, food, or fresh water, and some want help with other painful problems. The needs are overwhelming, and Nathan and Becky are viewed as a resource that can be tapped 24-7.

"So, Nathan," I said to my friend with real concern, "I am afraid that you and Becky are burning yourselves out. You are not going to last long without some margin and time for your own marriage and family." Nathan replied, "How can I take a day off around here? The lines never stop. I can't really put a sign on the fence that says, 'This is my day off—go away.'" I soon realized that Nathan and Becky have to take themselves away to have a day off. They can't take a day off and stay in their house, because people line up at their front gate looking for them. And believe me, the locals know whether anyone is home. Sitting in the house all day ignoring the folks at the gate would be cultural suicide in their village. The only way for them to get any margin is to drive several hundred miles on dirt roads to a nice, air-conditioned place where they can retreat. And you thought *you* had it rough!

Fortunately, most of us do not face the unique demands that Nathan and Becky have subjected themselves to. But you might be just as exasperated by the demands you face. Exactly what does it mean to be an accessible leader, and what boundaries do you need to set? How can you be more accessible, and why is that so important? And, finally, why is vulnerability so crucial in leadership today?

BEWARE OF THE IVORY-TOWER SYNDROME

Carlo Maria Giulini, former conductor of the Los Angeles Philharmonic, had a great way of talking about the blending of the leader with the team. A philharmonic orchestra is a team, and in order to produce beautiful music, they have to be *one in heart.* They have to be a connected team, and the conductor is the leader of that team. "My intention always has been to arrive at human contact without enforcing authority. A musician after all is not a military officer. What matters most is human contact. The great mystery of music making requires real friendship among those who work together. Every member of the orchestra knows that I am with him and her in my heart."[1]

When it comes to accessibility, beware of the ivory-tower syndrome. An ivory-tower leader is isolated from her team. Beware of hiding out in your corner office. That is so last century! I heard about a company where the leadership has opulent offices on a private top floor of the corporate headquarters, with a private elevator to get there. They have their own restaurant and their own health center. No "common folk" are ever allowed on the top floor where the leaders hang out. In the middle of the lobby is a spiral staircase with a brass chain draped across the access. The message to the employees is clear: "don't even think about going up there where the big shots are."

What kind of culture have these isolated leaders created? That is not hard to guess: a company with a total lack of trust between followers and leaders. Sadly, this old-style corporate culture still exists in a lot of places. Beware of the ivory-tower syndrome; effective leaders of the future will not make it a practice.

Accessibility is an important trait for every single leader. Whether you're type A or not, whether you're task-oriented or not, whether you're a people person or a to-do list person, you have to be accessible.

GENERATIONAL POWER DISTANCES COMPLICATE THINGS

My son Mark recently went to work for a baby boomer boss. He wrote me after a few months to tell me how much he loves this guy and his leadership. I asked him to tell me why. Here is part of his list:

- **He's collaborative rather than authoritarian.** I haven't had a lot of chances to work directly with him yet, but already I can tell that he isn't a top-down leader. He seems genuinely open to input and the collaborative environment that our generation appreciates.
- **My new CEO is accessible too.** He hosts regular meetings called "Coffee with the CEO" with the whole staff, and he shares his vision for the organization and lets anyone ask questions. This is also something important to our generation; we don't want a CEO off in some mahogany boardroom making all the decisions and bringing things down from "on high" … we want to be a part of what is going on. This kind of environment where he's sitting down with us over coffee resonates.

Have you heard the expression "power distance"? In the old days, there was a lot of power distance between leader and follower, between boss and employee, but over the decades, the power distance has shrunk and shrunk and shrunk. As a quick review in case this is new to you, there are five main generations alive today: builders, the silent generation, boomers, generation X, and millennials (aka generation Y). Here is how each generation views power distances between leaders and followers.

- **Builders and the silent generation were born before 1946:** They include the "Greatest Generation," who fought and died in World War II. This group generally keeps a huge power distance between boss and employees, between leader and followers—based on how things were in America in the 1930s and 1940s. Respect is speaking when spoken to and coming to the boss's big corner office only when summoned. The top brass does not mingle with the foot soldiers.

- **Boomers, born between 1946 and 1964:** Boomers grew up in the 1960s and '70s without the Internet, and they retain some of the builder values in human communication. I would say they generally have a medium power distance. You can't generalize on this generation very much; I know boomers who are just like builders and others who seem to have become millennials in their values and styles. But we boomers for sure have expected less power distance between us and our leaders ever since the 1960s, when we occupied the administration buildings at our universities during campus antiwar protests.

- **Generation X, born between 1965 and 1984:** This is a small generation, people in their thirties and forties today. Two of my four children are Xers. This generation expects a lot less distance between them and their leaders than any previous generation. They are much quicker to criticize their leaders openly.

- **Millennials, or generation Y, born between 1985 and 2005:** This is the massive generation in their twenties and thirties now entering the workforce. You are working with more and more of these people on your team. They are the 9/11 generation who have great expectations for themselves and those around them. They're actually a bigger generation than the boomers—over eighty million strong. For them, there is virtually no power distance between leader and follower. This generation has unlimited access to information and demands that of their leaders. They live in a 24-7 world and expect fast and immediate processing. In their worldview, there is nothing a leader should ever hold back from a follower.

Do you get the idea? Power distance is a real force to be considered if you are working with people who are not in your generation. As each generation comes along, it moves from formal to informal, and that affects what they demand in terms of accessibility. A great resource is the book *Sticking Points: How to Get 4 Generations Working Together in the 12 Places They Come Apart* by Haydn Shaw. Sometimes boomers are surprised by how millennials and Xers don't register power distance. It can feel threatening. Older people sometimes read this as a lack of respect, but that's not what's going on here. It's really a generational difference about the appropriate power distance between leader and follower.

> Power distance is a real force to be considered if you are working with people who are not in your generation.

Power distances also come into play big-time if you work with people from other cultures. We in America are a land of immigrants, and today many of them are from Asia and the Middle East. These cultures have a very different view of leadership than we do in America, especially when it comes to power distances. I love other cultures, and I've studied how leaders behave in other countries. I have a great example from what happened to me a few years ago in South Korea. I was teaching a one-week leadership training course in Seoul. In Korea, like China, Japan, and most Asian countries, there is still a huge power distance between leaders and followers, which goes back to the days when their leaders were emperors. It is hard to get that out of the culture! The compression of power distances in the arena of leadership in North America and Europe over the last forty years is just now happening in Asian cultures.

I was teaching this group of Koreans about the value of feedback, about emotional intelligence and how it's important for leaders to get an evaluation of their effectiveness by listening to their followers. The lecture came to a screeching halt. They started looking at me like deer in the headlights, as though they were asking, "What are you talking about?" I was sharing with them the journey of my recent comprehensive 360-degree evaluation that was performed by my board, soliciting input from my direct reports. They shared this with me: "We would *never, ever, ever* be allowed to give feedback to our leaders about how they're doing." I came to realize that many countries in Asia have face-saving cultures, and in those cultures, criticizing their boss would cause the boss to lose face. It would be considered disrespectful and an insult. Not allowable. Grounds for dismissal. Interesting, isn't it? Those leaders in Korea went on to tell me quietly behind closed doors, "I wish we could tell our leaders what we think of them. They are dictators!"

Most of you reading this book don't work in Korea; you work in America, and in America the power distances have gotten very small. But you might just have people on your team from Asia or the Middle East or Africa. If you are puzzled about how they react to you, it may be cultural.

I became the CEO of an international nonprofit in 1993, taking over from a member of the builder generation who had led the organization for twenty-three years. He was a wonderful man, but he had established a very formal office culture with coats and ties and formal titles. When I took over, my very first act was to abolish those coats and ties. I got rid of the designated CEO parking space. I remember the day I arrived at the office's parking lot and saw my name on a sign at the best parking spot closest to the back door. I grabbed the sign, pulled it out of the ground, and threw it in the Dumpster. I guess it was a boomer reaction to builder values. Then I told my team and everyone at the office, "I want you to call me 'Hans.' I am not 'Dr. Finzel.' I want you to address me by my first name." It was so hard for some of those people to do.

As the years went by, I was very encouraged when millennial and generation X members of my team told me, "I love how we feel that we have access to all the leadership. You guys work with us, you play with us, we feel like we can go to your office and talk to you, you come to our offices and talk to us ..." That was when I learned that accessibility is so important. When I asked the young staff how we could make our office an even better place to work, their number one suggested improvement was more communication with and access to the leaders. They wanted more accessibility.

WHAT FUELS AND FRUSTRATES YOUR YOUNG TEAMMATES

As my leadership of that ministry was coming to an end, I became more and more obsessed about helping the younger generations succeed in our organization. I wanted them to replace me and thrive. The challenge was that we were seventy years old as an organization, and generationally, we had to keep learning how to adjust. For every decade of your history, you are dragging another anvil of the old ways into the future. I was pleased to hand over the leadership to a generation Xer who's doing a great job. I like to think I plowed the ground for his success by making the corporate culture more youth oriented.

Here are some things I learned during my years of leadership about what fuels and what frustrates the younger generations we work with. *Fuel* is another word for *empower*. We either empower people who work with us—fuel them to want to charge forward—or we frustrate them. Can I assume that, if you are older, you would like to *fuel* them, not *frustrate* them? I hope that is true for you.

What *fuels* your younger-generation teammates? Ask for their input, offer recognition and praise, and help them see the context of what they are doing within the whole mission and purpose of the group. Give them feedback; answer their unspoken "How am I doing?" Another thing that fuels them is time spent with managers and leaders learning how their current work is making them more marketable for the future and providing them opportunities to learn new things. They also like fun at work, structured play, harmless practical jokes, lightheartedness, and flexible schedules: "Don't make me work nine to five or eight to four." Flexible work hours are huge for the young generation, as is telecommuting. Some boomers think they have to keep an eye on people to make sure they work hard. But *work is not a place you go to, it is a thing you do.* Two of our sons have jobs where they can telecommute some days. Their employers are smart to trust them to work from home.

What *frustrates* your young teammates in the workplace? The first frustration is being put in a place of isolation with no feedback. They want to know they are making a difference. They hate waiting in line and "paying their dues." What do I mean by that? It's this old builder and boomer mantra: "Stick around awhile, learn the ropes, and in five years, I'm going to give you something significant to do—but first you've got to pay your dues." I have news for you: they have zero interest in paying dues! They want to make a difference with their job immediately, with whatever they're doing. And don't expect them to do things the way you do them.

Other things that turn them off are processing change over a long period of time, leaders hiding out in their offices, leaders never being around, inflexibility about time and schedule, workaholism, being overly watched and scrutinized, and being in a controlling culture. Finally, the younger generations hate feeling pressured to convert to traditionalist behavior, and hearing disparaging comments about their generation's tastes, tattoos, and clothing styles.

Millennials and Xers have grown up with the ability to click a couple of keys and get what they want. They feel the same way when it comes to access to their leaders. They won't work very long on a team that erects large barriers between them and their leaders. They are not going to work for companies that have spiral staircases with brass chains.

ACCESSIBILITY IS NOT NEW

Even Jesus had an open-door policy. He had time for people, especially His inner circle of twelve. Isn't it amazing how much He got done in so little time? I would think He felt a lot of pressure to accomplish His assigned mission on earth. So why did He not seem rushed? Luke 4:40 says, "At

> Even Jesus had an open-door policy. He had time for people, especially His inner circle of twelve.

sunset, the people brought to Jesus all who had various kinds of sickness, and laying his hands *on each one*, he healed them."

Here's a similar story, from Matthew:

> News about him spread all over Syria, and people brought to him all who were ill with various diseases, those suffering severe pain, the demon-possessed, those having seizures, and the paralyzed; and *he healed them*. Large crowds … followed him. Now when Jesus saw the crowds, he went up on a mountainside and sat down. His disciples came to him, and he began to teach them. (4:24–5:2)

He was accessible to both His leadership team and to the people. When His team tried to push away the crowds, He usually rebuked them and remained accessible.

My wife, Donna, and her team leader, Jennifer, have been working together for fifteen years. Jennifer and her husband are wildly successful in their home-based healthy-lifestyle business. We know them up close and personally, and we respect them so very much as our leaders in this business. I don't know anybody who works harder than Jennifer. Last night, Donna and I were talking about how much we admire her. Donna commented, "She never seems stressed, distracted, or hurried when you talk to her." I know she has hundreds of people demanding thousands of things from her every week. She has built a massively successful business with very smart, demanding people on her team. I really admire her ability to be present in the moment and accessible to her team. In all the conversations I've had with her over the years, I can never remember a time when she's broken off the conversation with that stressed-out "I gotta go" kind of spirit. Somehow, I get the feeling that that is the way Jesus was as He walked the planet.

Paul, another of my favorite leaders in the New Testament, had a life-on-life style of leadership. Life-on-life is two people spending real, quality time together with the result that one life affects the other. Paul had no corner office, no ivory tower, no pulpit or lectern he hid behind. His work, his ministry as a leader, was life-on-life. He wrote to the Thessalonian church, "But we proved to be gentle among you, as a nursing mother tenderly cares for her own children. Having so fond an affection for you, we were well-pleased to impart to you not only the gospel of God [meaning the knowledge, the information] but also *our own lives,* because you had become very dear to us" (1 Thess. 2:7–8 NASB).

This is the same thing the symphony leader Carlo Maria Giulini was talking about: life-on-life. The more people you have on your team, the more pressure there is to isolate yourself, but don't get locked into that corner office or that ivory tower. Leadership is people work.

ACCESSIBILITY GUIDELINES TO KEEP YOUR LIFE SANE

Whether you are disciplined or scatterbrained, an introvert or extrovert, you have to make accessibility work in your life. Here are four guidelines I shared with Naomi after church that day when she was stressed about demands for her attention.

1. Respond quickly with a "yes," "no," or "later." It's never good to leave people hanging with silence. Any answer is better than no answer. Give people the respect they deserve by letting them know you got their message and you will get back to them. Never forget that your team takes much higher priority than the many random emails and messages you get from other people in your life.

2. Develop an accessibility schedule. Decide when each week you're going to be totally available to schedule team meetings, phone conversations, and one-on-one meetings. Be committed to stick to that schedule, and whenever people want you, you can pop them right into your calendar. Don't become a slave to the demands of others. Structure your interruptions. There were times in the life of Jesus when He had to be alone. He had to separate Himself from the demands of the crowd: "But Jesus often withdrew to lonely places and prayed" (Luke 5:16).

> Don't become a slave to the demands of others. Structure your interruptions.

3. Talk with your team about your style of work and theirs. It's amazing how unmet expectations create conflict on a team. It's best to verbalize your work style with one another so that you know how each of you approaches your work. Some of you are disciplined and highly organized, others fly like butterflies from one thing to the next. Both styles can be equally successful, and each needs to respect the other. I recommend using assessments such as StrengthsFinder and DISC, from which you can learn a lot about the styles of your team members.

4. Be proactive, not just reactive. Don't sit and wait for your team to contact you. Reactors never become big successes. Accessible leaders take initiative, accomplish great feats, and succeed with their dreams. No news is often bad news when you're trying to build a team. It's up to the leader to take the initiative to stay in touch with teammates to see how they're doing. Sometimes they allow things to fester. Other times they're drifting away and no longer engaging with what they should be doing. People need you, and if you have had no contact with your key leaders for a while, that is probably not good.

VULNERABILITY

Vulnerability and accessibility are joined at the hip. Together they make a powerful leadership force. I recently had the chance to hear talk show host and author Aisha Tyler speak at a convention I was attending. This accomplished speaker spoke to my gut and blew me away with her honesty. She said some important things about becoming a healthy person and a better leader, a lot of them having to do with being real and vulnerable about our flaws. She said, "Success is not the absence of failure; it is persistence through failure."[2] I love that.

We cannot create a world where we have no failure. When Tyler interviews famous people, she disarms them and gets them to admit their failures. Many of them failed miserably at times, but they persisted to the point of success. She reminded me that we're not perfect, and we shouldn't pretend to be perfect. In fact, that's what vulnerability is all about. Tyler quoted movie character Rocky Balboa, who famously said, "It's not how hard you hit, it's how hard you get hit and keep going." Failure is a prerequisite to success.

Vulnerability makes us more human. People love following leaders who are human! *As we make ourselves accessible, we also have to open up with vulnerability.* Vulnerability is a state of being open to injury or appearing as if you are. It might be emotional, like admitting that you're in love with someone who might only like you as a friend, or it can be literal, like the vulnerability of a soccer goal that's unprotected by the defensive players. Being vulnerable is showing weakness. It's showing your soft side, your brokenness. People don't like to work with people who pretend to be perfect.

Most of us don't naturally want to admit our flaws and short-comings, do we? We like to make people think we have our act together. There are a lot of reasons why we fear vulnerability: our personality, our upbringing, our fear of being discovered, our desire to keep up an image, pretension, pride—we can't admit our mistakes. We think, "People will find out I'm not perfect, and then they won't like me or accept me."

One of my new favorite authors is Brené Brown. Her message for leaders is about vulnerability. I highly recommend her books, including *Daring Greatly*. Here's what she said in a *Forbes* interview about how the courage to be vulnerable transforms the way we live, love, parent, and lead: "I spent a lot of years trying to outrun or outsmart vulnerability by making everything certain and definite, black and white, good and bad. My inability to lean into the discomfort of vulnerability limited the fullness of those important experiences that are wrought with uncertainty: Love, belonging, trust, joy, and creativity to name a few."[3]

I've always struggled with vulnerability. I'm a private person, and sometimes I come across as arrogant or prideful or "I'm too cool to talk to you." I hate the fact that I come across that way. The truth is the opposite. I finally came to grips with this and told my leadership team what I'm about to tell you. We were having issues working together, and I figured out I was partly to blame. I felt I had to open up in order to build trust, and once I unpacked my inner flaws for them, our relationship changed for the better overnight.

Here's what I confessed to my team: "I'm a type A personality," I began. "I'm driven to produce, and my family always judged me on what I did—*performance*—not on who I was becoming—*character*. We never shared on a personal level in my home, so I never learned about intimacy and vulnerability. I'm an INTJ on the Myers-Briggs Type Indicator; introverted and decisive, I thrive on getting things done by myself. And let's not forget that I'm a pragmatic German, and if you know any Germans, you know it can be tough to get under our skin. And this last one is a biggie: I'm an adult child of an alcoholic. My counselor, who helped me work through this, said that adult children of alcoholics follow these four rules: 1) they don't talk about what's important, 2) they don't feel, especially difficult emotions, 3) they don't trust people very much, and 4) they don't stop working, because they never feel that they're succeeding."

After my confession, you could have heard a cricket in the room. Then they began to respond. "Oh, now we get you. We thought you were being arrogant and did not care about us enough to open up. You are so hard to read. Thank you so much for helping us understand your struggles and why you act the way you do." That vulnerability led to more trust. They got what was going on inside of me. It was not the end of my struggles in being vulnerable, but it was the right direction for all of us to take.

I also got some counseling, and it helped me a lot. I think most of us could use a counselor or therapist. It can be very enlightening to pay a professional to listen deeply to our issues and help us get out of our thick skins. This is what getting a healthy EQ is all about. Don't be afraid to step up and open up—vulnerability is a powerful ally.

> Don't be afraid to step up and open up—vulnerability is a powerful ally.

I want to get back to Paul the apostle as we wrap up this chapter. Not only was he accessible to his people, he scored high in vulnerability—admitting how messed up he really was. He was saying, in effect, "I have no business being your leader. But God can use anyone willing to change." Here are some of Paul's words:

Here is a trustworthy saying that deserves full acceptance: Christ Jesus came into the world to save sinners—of whom *I am the worst.* (1 Tim. 1:15)

For I know that good itself does not dwell in me, that is, in my sinful nature. For I have the desire to do what is good, *but I cannot carry it out.* (Rom. 7:18)

For I am the *least of the apostles and do not even deserve to be called an apostle*, because I persecuted the church of God. (1 Cor. 15:9)

Paul was confessing, "I did a lot of bad stuff." Admitting all that failure did not disqualify him to lead. It actually endeared him to the people he led. We all have to lead people filled with flaws. As they see ours, it encourages them and gives them hope.

Trust me—this vulnerability stuff is a big deal. Brené Brown said, "If you think dealing with issues like worthiness and authenticity and vulnerability are really not worthwhile because there are more pressing issues, like the bottom line or attendance or standardized test scores, you're sadly, sadly mistaken. It underpins everything."[4]

ACTION POINTS AND DISCUSSION QUESTIONS

These four action points will help you learn to lead as it relates to the letter "A" in LEADERSHIP. Remember that the "A" stands for *accessibility*, and right on the heels of that idea is the partner practice of *vulnerability*. I am giving you two action points on accessibility and two on vulnerability.

1. Be sure you have times when you're accessible to your people. We don't get in life what we *want*; we get what we *schedule*. Try having an open-door (physical or electronic) policy according to your work style and schedule. Even if you are a highly spontaneous person, you need some structured alone time. Of course, a great way to spend time with your team is to have meals with them, go hiking, sip coffee, or, if you are in an office environment, manage by wandering around and talking to people in their cubicles. Great questions for discussion: How are each of us at planning for alone time versus time with people? Are we feeling like victims of the tyranny of the urgent? If so, what can we change in our routine?

2. When you need to be alone, structure it and let people know you'll get back to them. Boundaries are important. Henry Cloud and John Townsend's book *Boundaries: When to Say Yes, How to Say No to Take Control of Your Life* is a great resource. We do need boundaries, but we also need to have those times structured so that our team knows when we are accessible. And they need to understand why you're not available when you're not available—they need to know you have other stuff to do. You could set up a standard calendar with alone time blocked. Perhaps Tuesdays and Thursdays I hunker down and isolate myself for the work I need to do by myself. Or mornings, I get my alone-time work done, and afternoons are for interruptions and for my team. Discuss with one another what would work for you.

3. Don't pretend to be perfect or to have your entire act together. People don't like working for walled-off people who are pretenders. This is true in the church as well as in the business world. Hiding weaknesses does not build trust. Would people say that you are vulnerable with your weaknesses or are they off-limits? Do you always try to make yourself look together, or are you fine with showing your flaws? If you have the courage, these would be great questions to discuss with your team in a quiet, safe setting.

4. Watch the TED talk by Brené Brown on "The Power of Vulnerability." In 2010, Brené Brown gave a twenty-minute talk at her local TEDx event, TEDxHouston. That talk, "The Power of Vulnerability," has since become a web-video phenomenon, viewed over twenty-three million times as of this writing. People who have watched it say that her words on shame, vulnerability, and honesty moved them, inspired them, and helped them make change in their lives. This would be a great video to share with your team and discuss together. You can find it at TED.com.

4

"D" IS FOR DETERMINATION

Jack and I were the best of friends. We are the same age, and he is one of those friends you just enjoy being with. Our kids are the same ages, so we talk a lot about their growing pains. We have so much in common and laugh a lot. Well, I should say "we used to." We have not spoken in over a decade. Have you ever been betrayed by a good friend? Stabbed in the back? Jack betrayed me, and I never saw it coming. It felt like he became a different person when he deceived me after years of a great friendship. Isn't it funny how someone you would take a bullet for can be the one holding the gun?

Sometimes bad things happen to good people. It is impossible to "failure-proof" our lives, and that's certainly true of our journey as leaders. We all face tough times. Remember the words of Aisha Tyler: *Success is not the absence of failure; it is persistence through failure.* If I asked you to name the most discouraging times of your career, what would they be? Maybe some of you are in one right now. Are you going to make it through, or have you already decided to bail? One really nasty person can stop us dead in our tracks.

Here is how a great friendship turned into one of the greatest discouragements of my life. As I told you in the last chapter, I was the president of an international nonprofit ministry. Jack was very successful in ministry in New Jersey. I had gotten to know Jack through common interests in our professions. As a CEO, I was always looking for great new board members, so I figured, why not have this successful man on my board? We got along so well, it would be fun to see each other more often, and he would be a great new resource to the board. So we asked him, and he agreed to serve. After a few years, he became chairman of the board of directors. Everything was going great. It's nice having your friend as the board chair ... or so I thought. Really, what was I thinking?

Jack turned on me. It was subtle at first, but then became pronounced. Nothing is more painful than wounds inflicted by a friend. He turned on me because of certain values that I guess we did not share. The specifics are not important to the story. He came to the place where he didn't think I was up to his standards as the CEO. It was especially painful to me because I hate conflict— and certainly I did not think our differences warranted the end of our friendship. He was so convinced I was wrong that he sought to have me dismissed by the board. Then he circulated a letter full of lies about my character. Yes, my friend tried to have me fired. Fortunately, my board did not share his views. They supported me and got rid of him instead. The whole experience was painful, dark, and discouraging. I struggled to have the determination to go on. "Why is this happening to me?" I wondered.

I could not believe Jack ended our friendship over what I thought were minor matters. To him, though, they were major, and he drew a line in the sand as he ended our relationship. I did not live up to his expectations, so he gave up on me. It happens sometimes. Friendships blow up and end over differences in values, beliefs, or just plain cultural disagreements. What is *minor* in our minds is *major* in theirs.

The hardest thing about that journey was that I was not able to fix it for a long time. I'm a fixer. When Donna has something around the house that needs repairing, I am on it fast because I don't like things to be unresolved. I already told you I love to check things off lists. I hate conflict, and if there is conflict that affects me, I want to resolve it as soon as possible and check it off my emotional burden list. I think one reason I was so discouraged through the journey with Jack is that it took over a year for it to play itself out and get "fixed." You can't just check conflict off a list like you can replace a lightbulb in the bathroom. As this

> You can't just check conflict off a list like you can replace a lightbulb in the bathroom.

drama dragged on, I wondered if I could keep functioning as the leader while this side story played out. I had to wait on my board to resolve the situation, because pleading with my friend to come to reason utterly failed.

A young executive whom I mentor has been living with a lot of discouragement at his job for over two years. He works for a small company that is not doing well. It is filled with drama and dysfunction. This talented young man would love to leave, but the job market for what he can do is narrow, and he has a growing family to care for. So he stays stuck in a tough place that he cannot fix. I remind him constantly that he is developing character, and that someday he will see the silver lining of what he has been going through. He has endured and learned great lessons of determination. As a postscript to this story, as I was editing this chapter, I learned that this executive started a new career in an amazing new job just this week! He waited patiently for two years for the right thing to open up. I am so proud of his determination through very tough times. He is now making more money in a healthy environment, he loves his new boss, and he works only one mile from his home. How cool is that?

Legendary football coach Vince Lombardi once said, "The price of success is hard work, dedication to the job at hand, and the determination that whether we win or lose, we have applied the best of ourselves to the task at hand." In case you're not a football fan, how about cars? Famous race car driver Mario Andretti observed, "Desire is the key to motivation, but it's determination and commitment to an unrelenting pursuit of your goal—a commitment to excellence— that will enable you to attain the success you seek."

I was speaking to a group of young leaders recently on the topic of overcoming discouragement. They wanted to know how to stay determined and cope when things get rough. First, I asked them to help me make a list of all the discouraging things they might face as leaders. Together we brainstormed about the kinds of things that can stop us dead in our tracks. Here is their depressingly long list:

- Money problems
- Unmet expectations
- Unrealistic expectations—of others and myself
- Failure
- Lack of vision
- Illness
- Lack of support from family and friends
- Conflict
- Relationship stress
- Marriage problems
- Being misunderstood
- Betrayal
- Hard times
- Opposition
- Toxic workplace
- Comparison with others
- Personality problems
- Family background and upbringing

You and I both know this list is not exhaustive. Are you facing obstacles that are not even on my list? No leader gets a free pass and an easy ride. We just have to practice determination against

the many forces that try to stop us. I have always loved this Calvin
Coolidge quote on persistence:

> Nothing in this world can take the place of *per-*
> *sistence.* Talent will not; nothing is more common
> than unsuccessful men with great talent. Genius
> will not; unrewarded genius is almost a proverb.
> Education will not; the world is full of educated
> derelicts. Persistence and determination alone are
> omnipotent.

THE LEADERSHIP FORMULA

"Success is never final. Failure is seldom fatal. It is courage that
counts," said Winston Churchill, a leader who knew what setbacks
were all about. Determination requires courage, and courage is a
key quality of leaders who endure.

For many years, I have taught my classes a great formula for
successful leadership. This formula has three ingredients: Leader +
Followers + Situation = *Effective Leadership.*

> Leader + Followers +
> Situation = *Effective*
> *Leadership*

When all three ingre-
dients line up in a healthy
manner, you have powerful
leadership that really works.
Failure in any one of these three can create overall failure. You
can be a great leader but in a tough situation and things don't
work. Or your situation may be great but your followers are weak.

Sometimes the followers are great and the situation is perfect, but there are problems in the leader. I have seen leaders struggle in each of these three elements, with things *not* working out well because of 1) their own inner problems, 2) followers on their team who are not working out, or 3) a really tough situation in which to lead.

Let's think for a moment about the various combinations of this leadership formula. If all three elements line up right, you will experience effective leadership. If you are failing, it might not be your fault. I love it when the leadership stars align. Sadly, it does not happen as often as you might think. If you sense you are doing everything right as a leader but are still failing, then you may need to turn your attention to improving your team (or getting a new one) or changing your situation.

Let's turn the microscope on your own leadership. Sometimes you are the main problem. It's not the followers or the situation. You're struggling with yourself, you're your biggest enemy, and you are the victim of self-sabotage. In fact, you can have great followers and a great situation but be unable to pull yourself out of the funk you're in or the self-sabotage of your addictions. Sometimes, people like this become great pretenders even as others around them wonder why things are not going well. Susan, whose lack of EQ I discussed in chapter two, is an example of a leader with a blind spot that is hindering her effectiveness. In her case, the followers and the situation are not the problem.

If you know that *you* are the problem, I encourage you to practice courageous leadership and get some professional help. You might need to see a counselor as I did when I struggled with family heritage challenges. Or hire an executive coach who can walk with you in your journey. You may not be able to control your followers or the situation, but you are the captain of your own leadership.

I love the leadership determination of General Colin Powell. I consider Powell to be a courageous leader, and I wish he had run for president. He led the U.S. military and served four U.S. presidents well. Can you imagine the determination he had to exhibit to survive and thrive? He once said, "A dream doesn't become reality through magic; it takes sweat, determination, and hard work."

OVERCOME RESISTANCE

Have you ever felt as though there are unseen forces holding you back? That as much as you want to improve and become more successful, something keeps you in the old ruts? I have talked so far in this chapter about *determination* and *courageous leadership*. The third thing I want to mention is *overcoming resistance*, an invisible force that holds us back from making significant progress. Michael Hyatt's podcast "How to Overcome the Resistance" first exposed me to this concept and the writings of Steven Pressfield. Pressfield has called resistance "that invisible destructive force that opposes you any time you try to do something significant or make an improvement in any area of your life."[1] In his *The War of Art*, he shared his struggle to become a screenwriter in Hollywood. "What does that have to do with me?" you might be wondering. Pressfield's book would be helpful for anyone who does not punch a clock and work a 9-to-5 job. Whether you are a writer, artist, or musician, or you're building your own business or ministry and have to motivate yourself to do your work, resistance will attack you.

Have you ever felt this resistance? I do all the time. Resistance convinces you to stay in bed instead of getting up to face the day. Resistance has you focus on that one critical comment instead of the ninety-nine positive comments people made about you and your work. Resistance is staying home instead of going out. It's getting the closet organized instead of getting out there and doing those high-payoff activities that you know you should do. Resistance cannot be seen, touched, heard, or smelled. It's a restrictive, negative force; its aim is to distract us, to discourage us, and to stop us—dead in our tracks. The more important our work is, the more resistance will show up to stop us.

The many people who work in a job with regular office hours *have* to show up. They might not be working, but they are at their desks. I left that kind of structure four years ago when I went to work for myself. I am my own boss and have created a new company and nonprofit to pursue my calling to help leaders. I love the

> Resistance cannot be seen, touched, heard, or smelled. It's a restrictive, negative force; its aim is to distract us, to discourage us, and to stop us—dead in our tracks.

freedom of my new career, but I do face resistance. If I don't get out of bed in the morning, nobody cares. Well, maybe Donna cares; she wants me to get up and going. If I don't motivate myself, nobody else will. I can find so many trivial things to do to waste my time. Some of you may not have issues with self-motivation, but others totally get what I am talking about.

If you live in the kind of profession I am describing, you know how easy it is to waste time doing unimportant things while your art does not get created or your message does not get delivered. The unseen forces of resistance try to keep you from gaining momentum. You fight fear that never goes away. Whether you like it or not, the battle must be fought anew every single day. Resistance aims to stop you, to kill you. It targets the epicenter of your being, your genius, your soul, the unique and priceless gift you were put on this earth to give and no one else has.

So what should you do? Recognize that this problem is real. Get going, do the work, and the feelings will follow. The best way to fight resistance is action—massive action. The greatest way to combat procrastination and gloom and fear is to act and move out. Haven't you seen this time and time again? If you start doing the work, the feelings will follow. I find that is true every single day of my life. Once I commit to forward action, the feelings eventually join up with me, and I have a delightfully successful day.

> The best way to fight resistance is action—massive action.

THREE PRIME EXAMPLES OF SUCCESS THROUGH DETERMINATION

Before I finish this chapter, I want to illustrate successful determination with three of my favorite stories about famous people. Seeing other people succeed despite great opposition is encouraging. These stories of success have a lot to teach us. Some of you might think, what a strange combination of people: Colonel Sanders, Nelson Mandela, and Moses. You'll see the common thread of determination and courageous leadership as you read on.

Colonel Sanders. This is a story of determination and success late in life. While trying to interest others in his recipe for chicken, Harland Sanders, who would later become the founder of Kentucky Fried Chicken, was turned down over a thousand times. He drove from town to town calling on restaurant owners, often sleeping in his car. He remained persistent, strongly believing his secret recipe would eventually pay off. Talk about resistance—everywhere he went people told him, "We don't need a chicken store—nobody's going to buy just chicken." But his persistence and confidence in himself and his recipe finally paid off in a big way, and he found success when he was sixty-five years old. His tenacity is inspiring. The lesson here is don't let resistance tell you it's too late to start over. Who would follow a leader my age? Why should people hear my voice? I travel the world, and everywhere I go there are Kentucky Fried Chicken restaurants. The colonel never shared his secret recipe, but he did share his recipe for success: *never quit, always believe in yourself, be patient, and be positive.*

Nelson Mandela. This is a story of starting something new late in life after waiting decades to fulfill a calling you know you have but which circumstances prevent. The world not too long ago mourned the death of this great world leader. One of Nelson Mandela's greatest achievements did not happen until he was seventy-two years old and had been released after spending twenty-six years in prison. I think he had always been a great leader, but he got stuck in a lousy situation he did not deserve, forcibly separated from his followers. Then everything lined up for Mandela. He was elected president of South Africa four years after he was released from prison, and he served in that position for five years. He experienced an additional decade of prominence and influence before his declining health forced a full retirement. Mandela rescued South Africa from civil war and destruction and put the country back together. He was a tremendous leader who lived out courageous leadership and persistence. All the years he was in prison, he believed that he would be released one day and that he would have the opportunity to bring about a dramatic change for his country.[2]

Moses. At the outset of this chapter I told you a story about the chairman of my board who was out to get me. It was a very painful sabotage. During that time, I was drawn to study the life of Moses in the Old Testament. I knew he was a great leader who faced more discouragement and opposition than almost anybody I know of in history. I think I was drawn to him because I thought, *My situation is not as bad as his was—maybe he can help me learn how to cope with betrayal and not give up.* Going back to my leadership equation, I think Moses was a great leader who was asked by God to lead a horrible group of followers in a rotten situation. Through it all, for forty years till he was finished, he never gave up!

In the New Testament book of Hebrews, we read just how flaky his followers were. Hebrews 3:8–10 says, "Do not harden your hearts as you did in the rebellion, during the time of testing in the wilderness, where your ancestors tested and tried me, though for forty years they saw what I did. That is why I was angry with that generation; I said, 'Their hearts are always going astray, and they have not known my ways.'" Talk about lousy followers! I admire the determination and courageous leadership that Moses displayed.

The last great act of leadership is to develop a good team who can become your successors. Moses developed Joshua and Caleb as his short list to succeed him. When he turned things over to Joshua, he threw down the gauntlet of courage, persistence, and determination.

> The last great act of leadership is to develop a good team who can become your successors.

Here's what he said: "Be strong and courageous, for you must go with this people into the land that the LORD swore to their ancestors to give them, and you must divide it among them as their inheritance. The LORD himself goes before you and will be with you; he will never leave you nor forsake you" (Deut. 31:7–8).

THE TWO CHOICES

I am a huge fan of entrepreneur Jim Rohn. He understood all about determination, resistance, and courageous leadership. One of my favorite things he wrote highlights the "D" for *determination* in LEADERSHIP:

> Each of us has two distinct choices to make about what we will do with our lives. The first choice we can make is to be less than we have the capacity to be. To earn less. To have less. To read less and think less. To try less and discipline ourselves less.
>
> These are the choices that lead to an empty life. These are the choices that, once made, lead to a life of constant apprehension instead of a life of wondrous anticipation.
>
> And the second choice? To do it all! To become all that we can possibly be. To read every book that we possibly can. To earn as much as we possibly can. To give and share as much as we possibly can. To strive and produce and accomplish as much as we possibly can. All of us have the choice.

To do or not to do. To be or not to be. To be
all or to be less or to be nothing at all.[3]

ACTION POINTS AND DISCUSSION QUESTIONS

Let's get back to that group of young leaders I was training on the topic of overcoming discouragement. They wanted to know how to stay determined and how to cope when things get rough. This is the list of six recommendations I shared with those students. When things slow down, or opposition throws you for a loop, try these recommendations. If you are like me and struggle with resistance, these things work to get you back in the game.

1. Try this first: trust God. I know, that's easy to say but hard to do. Believe me, I know that very much firsthand! If you're a follower of Him, that's the first thing you ought to do. I read and claim Philippians 1:6 almost every morning: "There has never been the slightest doubt in my mind that the God who started this great work in you would keep at it and bring it to a flourishing finish on the very day Christ Jesus appears" (THE MESSAGE).

When I left the security of a 9-to-5 job and launched out on my own, it was scary. If you are leaving a day job for a dream job of working as your own boss, you know what I am talking about. God gave me a few very precious promises that I hung on to during my transition toward a career filled with passion. Here is one: "I wait quietly before God, for my victory comes from him.

He alone is my rock and my salvation, my fortress where I will never be shaken" (Ps. 62:1–2 NLT).

2. Trust yourself. "Courage is being scared to death and saddling up anyway," said John Wayne. Sometimes the biggest challenge is to consistently *believe in you*. Our biggest enemy is ourselves. We self-sabotage ourselves, and we don't believe in ourselves. And, of course, there are the other people who try to make us small. Oprah Winfrey has said, "Every time you suppress some part of yourself or allow others to play you small, you are in essence ignoring the owner's manual your creator gave you and destroying your design."[4] You've got to learn to believe in yourself. I read a series of affirmations about myself every morning to help me have the right frame of mind. They include some verses from the Bible that mean a lot to me. These affirmations remind me of who God says I am and who I know I am when I am at my best. I wrote them with great thoughtfulness at a time when I was thinking straight about who I am. I really do believe in myself, so I remind myself that I have a lot to offer the planet. Try this practice yourself. I even recorded my affirmations so that I can listen to them in my car or while walking or riding my bike.

3. Remember that "this too shall pass." This is something I tell my children all the time when they face discouragement. Tough times usually don't last; troubles and discouragements usually pass. You know it will not be this way forever. Sometimes you just have to hunker down and wait for troubles to go away.

If they do not go away after a very long time of waiting and suffering, you might have to make a change. In that case, I recommend *Necessary Endings* by Henry Cloud. This book will show you that at times you need to bring something to an end—a relationship, a position, a situation, or anything else that keeps you down.

4. Be connected with a community of people who will help you keep going. The founder and president of our Juice Plus+ business, Jay Martin, always exhorts us to "find a buddy." It is hard not to get discouraged working by yourself, but with a buddy, you can keep each other moving forward. This is not a new idea; it is found in one of the oldest books of the Bible. Ecclesiastes 4:12 says, "Though one may be overpowered, two can defend themselves. A cord of three strands is not quickly broken."

So why stop at one buddy? Look how strong a cord of three strands is! Be part of a mastermind group or a men's group or a women's group. Find people you can collaborate with. Donna has joined a group of women who are studying Kathrine Lee's *Ultimate Source* life-coaching material together (www.ultimatesource.tv). This is a great example of a community of women learning together and helping one another grow in their leadership. If you are in the kind of business that has meetings and conventions, you have to go. Sometimes you need the meetings, and many times the meetings need you. When you are consistently connected to a group of other people in your work, they can lift you up when you are down, and vice versa. For those of us working on our own, this is a huge advantage in overcoming resistance. It's also known as *accountability*.

5. Read or listen to *Do the Work* by Steven Pressfield. Please get this book if the section on *resistance* resonated with you. I enjoyed the audiobook version. Listen to and talk about some of the chapters with your loved ones and your team. See how it can help you understand the hidden forces that might be holding you back every day.

6. Commit to massive action. Nothing can shift your mind-set and spirit faster than movement. Get going, do the work, and the feelings will follow. The greatest way to combat procrastination, gloom, and fear is to act and move out. Feelings follow like a caboose when the engine of work is activated.

"E" IS FOR EFFECTIVE COMMUNICATION

We sat in a circle around a large conference table in Vienna, Austria, and began to talk about the vision of our team and where we were going. The consultant did what a lot of good consultants do. He asked us each to write down the core purpose of our organization on a 3x5 index card. What were we in the business of providing our users? What was our reason for existing? Ten quiet minutes passed as we all pondered and wrote our answers. Then we went around the circle and each of us read what we had written. No two of us said the same thing, and some of us were really, really far afield from the others. No wonder there was so much chaos among us. And our leader was mad at us for not giving the "right" answer! He *thought* that what was in his head resided in ours just as clearly, but that could not have been further from the truth.

George Bernard Shaw said, "The single biggest problem in communication is the illusion that it has taken place." Donna and I learned this firsthand when living overseas as a young married couple. We had the privilege of working in Vienna for a decade. Two of our four children were born there. What a great city to start your working career! When Donna and I arrived, we were one of the first five families to start a dynamic new project based there. Within a couple of years, we were up to about thirty families. It was so exciting to be part of a vibrant, entrepreneurial ministry start-up. Our mission was to train church and ministry leaders behind the Iron Curtain in communist Eastern Europe. Since these leaders had no access to seminaries, we launched a secret "seminary on wheels" that took the training to them.

About three years into our project, we began to sense major growing pains. We invited a management consultant to come in and spend a day with our top leadership. That's how we found ourselves around that conference table, filling out 3x5 cards and learning that no two of us thought the same thing. There was a *lot* of confusion about our purpose and direction. Like the strings of a guitar that lose their tuning, we had lost our harmony as a leadership group. *Never assume that everyone is on the same page with you.*

You know you're in trouble when the top leadership team is confused about fundamental issues, such as the core purpose of the group's existence and where it should be going. Our team did not spend enough time making sure we were all singing off the same page of the hymnal. Our leader was the founder, and many founders fall into the trap of assuming that the vision in their heads is crystal clear and oozes by osmosis into every new person who joins the team.

This communication problem was exacerbated by the other big problem on our team: *hallway decision making*. Our small team all worked in the same office, on the same floor, down the hall from one another. We decided everything in the hallways. When a problem came up, someone would lean their head out the door and ask, "Hey, what do we do about this?" Pretty soon, we were all out in the hall making policy and setting direction—and not bothering to write anything down.

What was going wrong here? These were natural growing pains. There was a lot of confusion about what we were going to do next. We had an oral culture, and we were guilty of routine hallway decision making. This was fine when you were new and small and all working at the same location: "Hey, I've got this problem; let's all gather in the hall and fix it." The problem was that because nothing was written down, there was no process, and confusion began to reign as more people were added to the mix. People who were not there at the beginning did not have the history of what happened in those hallways. Others joined the team at remote locations and in other cities. They were left to guess and wonder about a lot of things. Because of our success, we outgrew our offices and no longer shared the same hallways!

How would your team do with this exercise? Would your 3x5 cards all look the same? A small team can get away with an oral culture for a while. This is true of small businesses, new church plants, and most start-ups. But as you grow and succeed, not everybody can fit in a hallway anymore. Whether you like it or not, when you grow bigger and when your team is decentralized, you have to formalize communication systems and decision making. You've got to get out of the hallway. Things must get organized, and decisions have to be put on paper.

THE SECOND "E" IN LEADERSHIP

Did you notice that the letter "E" appears twice in LEADERSHIP? When I was mapping out this book, looking for the right words to put with each of the letters, I decided the first "E" would be for EQ, and this second "E" would stand for a topic equally important to your leadership: *effective communication.*

In this chapter, I will share four things that will help launch you as a great communicator. First, why is communication so important for you as a leader? So many people feel that their leaders leave them in the dark. Good communication skills will solve that problem. Second, I will tell you why you have to set a high priority on communicating often with your team. Third, I will share with you the content of your communication as a leader—what I would call the building blocks of great communication. And fourth, I'm going to leave you with five action steps you can apply right away to communicate effectively with your people.

I mentioned before that I asked my podcast listeners for feedback as I was building this book. I wanted them to answer the question "What is one of the ten essential skills every new leader must master?" I've received some quality feedback regarding successful communication in leadership. Tim said, "Effective communication is essential in all relationships. Be able to set clear expectations (sending) and be a good listener (receiving)."[1] Reverend Gibbs of Tallahassee, Florida, remarked, "I believe the single most important skill is communication."[2] So many other factors come to mind, but I think we probably can all agree that a leader's ability to communicate with clarity and consistency is vital.

Your team cannot read your mind. That was the problem with our leader in Vienna. He assumed that what was in his mind was in ours. We never communicate as much as we should as leaders—or as much as *we think we do*. All the followers I talk to seem

> Communication is the lifeblood running through the veins of your team.

hungry to hear from us more often. The funny thing about communication is that we assume too much. We think our team has absorbed what we are thinking without us actually telling them. Communication is the lifeblood running through the veins of your team. The better you communicate, the healthier you are. In his book *Leadership Is an Art*, Max De Pree wrote,

A corporation's values are its life's blood. Without effective communication, actively practiced, without the art of scrutiny, those values will disappear in a sea of trivial memos and impertinent reports. There may be no single thing more important in our efforts to achieve meaningful work and fulfilling relationships than to *learn and practice the art of communication.*[3]

PEEK BELOW THE WATERLINE

I thought everything was fine between Brian and me. We had been on the same leadership team for years, and I thought he respected my leadership. But lately, he had become an iceman. When we talked, his answers were very short. When I probed him about whether something was wrong, he gave the great answer that we so often use, "No, everything is *fine.*" There was something going on under the waterline that I had to figure out.

When you talk to people about big issues that affect them, things around them that are going to change, you have to look below the waterline. Both the conscious and the subconscious are simultaneously at work in people's minds, processing what's going on. It's not only in their minds; it's in their hearts. Often, what you don't see and what you don't hear and what you don't pick up from them is what will kick you in the rear.

An old farmer once said, "Go slow. People are a lot like horses. They don't like to be startled or surprised. It causes deviant behavior."

You can almost picture the weathered face of the man saying that, can't you? He's probably chuckling at the thought of a vicious kick he once took from an old mare he startled. As many old-timers are, he was right: go slow, because people don't like to be startled, and that obviously applies to the issue of bringing about change.

There is never a time when communication is more important than when you are in a process of implementing big changes. I sat down face-to-face with each of my senior-level leaders as I was going about a reorganization of our leadership structure. Brian had been in our organization for decades, and I spent considerable time with him sharing some of the major changes going on and how they would affect him.

> There is never a time when communication is more important than when you are in a process of implementing big changes.

When I started as CEO, I had fourteen people reporting to me. That is way too many for any leader. As we were growing and expanding around the world, my board said to me, "Hans, you've got too many people reporting to you; you've got to cut it down to be effective." So I had to go through a painful process of selecting who would stay on my team and who would go—who would still be at the table and who would be invited to leave. I had to break the news to Brian that he was no longer going to have a chair with the top leadership team. He was actually going to report to one of the people who, up to that point, had been his peer. I eventually got my direct reports down to seven.

In such highly charged, vulnerable moments, when there are big issues going on, there is no substitute for face time. I knew this would be a delicate situation for Brian because these changes involved him moving into a totally different place in the organization. I knew that many circumstances surrounding the decision would be difficult for him. I knew that he would feel demoted. I also knew it was best for him, because I knew what he really liked to do and I realized that, whether he knew it or not, this would free him up to pursue his passion. I might have seen that clearly, but it was extremely hard for him to grasp.

In a commitment to clear personal communication with Brian, I carefully explained the decisions and why I had made them. I allowed plenty of time for feedback and questions. When the conversation was over, I was surprised at Brian's reaction. He took it very well, calmly, almost stoically. I remember thinking to myself, "This doesn't add up. Either this guy is a lot more mature than anybody I've ever met or something else is going on." In fact, I was so bewildered that I told him to go home and think about it and asked to meet with him again in a couple of days. I was convinced that a whole minefield of issues was under the waterline—issues that would soon erupt onto the surface. Brian assured me, "It's fine. I got it. No problem. We don't need to meet again."

I forced that second meeting a couple of days later. And my gut was right. Brian went home that night and barely slept. Sure enough, issues exploded from under the surface within twenty-four hours. As he was mulling over the implications of my decision in his heart, the ramifications came: "What are people going to think? What am I going to do? I'm no longer as important as I was. I have been demoted." He was reeling with emotional confusion. He told me he got up at 3:00 a.m. and wandered the streets of his neighborhood, extremely upset about what I had shared with him. To say the least, he was very angry with me.

Fortunately, I followed up on my intuition. It's always a good idea to follow your gut perceptions about the people you work with. Leaving things alone in hopes that they will resolve themselves is never a good idea. We scheduled the follow-up meeting and finally got to the real issues at hand. I learned a valuable lesson from that episode: *don't assume people are going to take what you tell them at face value*. Brian did feel devalued. He said, "Gosh, I'm just not as important as I used to be; this is the end of my career. My colleagues are more valued than I am. I'm supposed to go forward, not backward."

The story of Brian has a happy ending. Years later,

> Don't assume people are going to take what you tell them at face value.

he is in charge of a major area of the world for the ministry, and this has given him the opportunity to spend more time in that part of the world. He finally appreciated the fact that he didn't have to waste time at the home office in all those long meetings that we leaders have to do. He circled back around and said to me, "You know, Hans, that was a great decision—the right decision. It hurt me at the time, but you actually launched me toward my heart and passion. Today, I love what I am doing, and I am doing what I'm best at. Thank you." Pretty cool, huh?

Did you hear about the rebellious little girl who was forced to have a time-out and sit in the corner for an hour? She told her mommy, "I might be sitting down on the outside, but I am standing up on the inside." If you as the leader ignore below-the-waterline issues, it almost always comes back to hit you. Regarding Brian, what would have happened if I'd never had that follow-up meeting? I would have wrongly concluded that everything was fine, checked that off the list, and moved on to the next problem. Somewhere down the road, there would have been an explosion. Something very negative would have happened. It could have been an obvious, in-my-face blowup or a quiet, subversive, passive-aggressive reaction, which people often have when they don't agree with their leaders. If there's no follow-up conversation, then there's no healing. They might look like they are sitting down in submission, but inside they are standing up. Sooner or later, that inner wound is going to cause great damage to the unity of your team.

THE PRIORITY OF COMMUNICATING

In *The Four Obsessions of an Extraordinary Executive,* Patrick Lencioni talks about the huge problem we busy leaders have with trying to focus. With so much to do and our team demanding so much of our time, how can we be sure we are doing the right things every day? Two of Lencioni's four obsessions are *gaining organizational clarity* and *communicating that clarity*. Those were the exact things lacking in our young team in Vienna. Here's what Lencioni says:

> Within companies that effectively over-communicate, employees at all levels and in all departments understand what the organization is about and how they contribute to its success. They don't spend time speculating on what executives are really thinking, and they don't look for hidden messages among the information they receive. As a result, there is a strong sense of common purpose and direction, which supersedes any departmental or ideological allegiances they may have.[4]

Donna's team leader, Jennifer, has a regular conference call on Monday mornings with her team leaders scattered all over the country. Sometimes I am home and listen in as Jennifer is leading a collaborative mastermind hour. She's guiding, asking questions, listening, and sharing the latest success strategies for their business. I always think to myself, "She is doing the right thing with these Monday-morning calls." She is staying in touch with her leaders and they know what is going on. There is no confusion about direction, priorities, or where their leader stands this week. As of this writing, Jennifer has about twenty high-octane leaders on that call every Monday, and their success is inspiring. Jennifer never asks her team to do anything she is not out there doing herself.

The opposite type of leader is an isolated leader, one who is fueling the flames of discord because people are reading into their work environment things that are not even there. Neglected followers provide very little usefulness to the cause.

Learn to overcommunicate by a factor of ten. Speak, rinse, and repeat. Everyone you work with struggles with tech clutter. The emails, texts, blogs, IMs, Facebook and Twitter posts, and you name it create background noise that makes it tough for your message to get through. You will never overcommunicate. I don't think that is possible. Many effective leaders I know have Monday-morning stand-up meetings with their team just to touch base and start the week on the same page.

> Learn to overcommunicate by a factor of ten.

A wounded wife told her husband, "You never tell me you love me." "Look," he replied impatiently, "I told you that that I loved you the day we got married. If I change my mind, I will let you know." A team can feel just as neglected as that spouse. Vision leaks. Communication of the vision with your team is critical to repeat over and over. The most carefully crafted messages rarely sink deeply into the receiver's consciousness after only one pronouncement. Our minds are too cluttered, and any one communication has to fight hundreds of other messages for attention.

Here's a shocker: not everyone is reading your email updates! I have a friend who was working as a consultant to help a pastor communicate better. The pastor thought he was communicating quite well. He sent a weekly email update to the congregation. Everybody in the congregation played nice and gave the church office their email addresses. His plan for communication was simple: "I'm going to write you once a week to tell you what's going on in the church." He thought for sure he was going to get a big gold star for being such a great communicator!

You probably know what's coming if you know anything about email blasts. He was stunned, absolutely crushed, when the consultant went into the email account dashboard and showed him that on average only 23 percent of the church members opened the email. And you probably know that even an "open" does not constitute a "read." He was devastated. Twenty-three percent? He reacted like Rodney Dangerfield: "I don't get no respect." He was angry at his people for not reading his missives.

A national average for people actually opening emails is something like 15 percent. He was at 23 percent, and he was devastated. What is the moral of this story? You can't just communicate through one medium to your people. You have to communicate through various channels over and over again. If you want to practice what Lencioni advocates, you have to maintain organizational clarity, and you have to obsess on communicating that clarity with your team. A little later in this chapter I will talk about the various avenues you can use—beyond face-to-face, emails, and video.

WHAT MUST I COMMUNICATE TO MY TEAM?

I'm devoting the third part of this chapter to exploring what exactly to communicate. First of all, I encourage you to adopt this principle: *never assume that anyone knows anything.* You cannot overcommunicate. So what exactly should you be talking about during times when you interact with your team?

I recommend four basic ingredients of good communication from leaders to their team:

1. Communicate the big, hairy vision. Be able to articulate the grand vision in an elevator speech. Everybody on the leadership team should be writing the same thing on that 3x5 card. If they're not, you've got work to do. Your people have to be constantly reminded about the dream: "Tell us again—where are we going?" The whole leadership team must be on the same page, singing off the same page of the hymnbook. You all have to get that elevator speech or the bullet points or whatever you use to communicate the grand vision down cold. Everyone must be able to answer the question "Where are we going and what do we stand for?" Practice it with one another. Have new team members work on it and recite it back to you.

2. Communicate concrete strategies and plans. Your team needs direction. They need to know where you are heading and what you expect of them. People hate surprises. Your team loses momentum when it is left in the dark. The more they know about the plans that are affecting them, the better. There are so many ways to communicate—Facebook, Twitter, blogs, emails, Skype, Zoom, Voxer, and conference calls. Let your team know what's going on, what's on the horizon, and what you are busy doing this week.

3. Be sure to communicate confrontations and corrections when needed. Communication is not just about good news. Sometimes, it is about things your team members are doing wrong. I am naturally a conflict avoider, but I learned the hard way that good leadership requires having tough conversations at times. And when you have to have those tough conversations, be clear about what you are getting at. Many of us are too soft and beat around the bush when it comes to confrontation. As Winston Churchill said, "If you have an important point to make, don't try to be subtle or clever. Use a pile driver." (I'm not sure what a pile driver is. I'm thinking it's probably a sledgehammer.) Be clear. Clarity even in confrontation is one of the biggest responsibilities of leadership. But also be measured in your approach. A Chinese proverb says, "Do not remove a fly from your neighbor's face with a hatchet." Be very clear but not cruel. A spoonful of sugar does help the medicine go down.

4. Troll for questions from your team—never make communication all one-way. Recently, Amazon experienced a firestorm, with employees going to social media complaining about terrible workplace conditions. The CEO, Jeff Bezos, heard these rumblings and responded to a *New York Times* article about the work conditions. He wrote a memo to his people: "The article doesn't describe the Amazon I know or the caring Amazonians I work with every day. But if you know of any stories like those reported, I want you to escalate to HR. You can also email me directly at jeff@amazon.com. Even if it's rare or isolated, our tolerance for any such lack of empathy needs to be zero."[5]

I thought that was a bold move for Jeff Bezos. I don't know the whole truth, whether these were just a few disgruntled employees or if this was a huge problem in the biggest retail company on planet Earth. But it's a healthy sign when the top leader says, "I want to hear from you if there's a problem."

> It's a healthy sign when the top leader says, "I want to hear from you if there's a problem."

Look for problems, allow disagreements, and be vulnerable and transparent when questions come. Create a culture that allows for good, healthy conflict. This goes back to embracing doubt, which I covered in chapter one under "Four Factors of Doubt."

Honestly, sometimes we have too many meetings but too little communication. Communication takes place when the person has finally understood what you've tried to get across and she can repeat back to you what you said. I first learned these lessons in grad school a long time ago back in Dallas, Texas. One of my professors, Dr. Paul J. Meyers, said, "Communication, the human connection, is the key to personal and career success."

ACTION STEPS AND DISCUSSION QUESTIONS

Learn to sharpen your communication strategies with these five concrete action steps:

1. Share the vision, rinse, and repeat. Assume that people don't understand where you're heading. Assume they have not gotten it. Remember you are constantly getting new people on board. Repeat the vision in different settings and from different angles. Ask your team next time you are together, "On a scale of one to ten, how well do we communicate our vision as a team?" Depending on how you score, talk about which ideas from this chapter you could try to implement.

2. Remember that face time makes or breaks your communication with your team. Make sure you meet face-to-face (or via video on the web) with key decision makers and give them time to talk to you. Your communication needs to be bidirectional. Are you sure you know what is going on in their lives, not just in their work? Don't program every minute. Troll for issues under the waterline. That's part of the responsibility of a leader.

3. Communicate in writing, not just orally. Use emails, your blog, Twitter, video, audio, Zoom, Facebook, your website, and team meetings. Communicate, communicate, and communicate some more on a regular basis, not once a month. List the various ways you can communicate to your organization. Ask your team what type of communication they like best when hearing from you. Try sending out a short weekly video update to your team via email to let them know what you are excited about this week.

4. Try the 3x5 card exercise. You can do this on the phone or as a face-to-face exercise. When you have your next team meeting, have everyone get a 3x5 card and write the answer to this question: "*We exist for the purpose of …*" Then have everyone share what he wrote on his card. No cheating. No changing their answers after other people have taken their turn. When everyone else has had a turn, give your answer. Then discuss why you wrote what you did. Some of you work in organizations and businesses where the vision and mission are already clearly stated from the corporate home office. In that case, it is important for your team to memorize those statements and be able to share them freely. If they don't understand the vision and mission, it's a great teaching moment for you.

5. Listen to my podcast "Care Enough to Confront." I mentioned in this chapter that many of us are conflict avoiders. Ask your team what they think about this subject. How many would say that they find it tough to confront people with negative behavior? Listen to my podcast as a team exercise and then discuss it in team training. The podcast gives concrete suggestions on how to confront without hurting people or damaging your team (www.hansfinzel.com/21).

6

"R" IS FOR RESILIENCE

My favorite cherry tree in our front yard finally died. It seems like every time we had a strong windstorm or heavy snow, it lost another branch. I hated to lose it, but the day finally came when we had to cut it down. Once the tree was lying in pieces on our front yard, I understood why it kept breaking. It was dead inside, totally dried out and infested with ants. When the winds and snows arrived, of course it snapped. A vibrant, living, healthy tree bends with the elements—that is its design. But once it dies inside, it snaps and breaks into pieces as storms are thrown at it.

Teams and organizations are very much like our cherry tree. So are leaders. If they are alive and thriving on the inside, exhibiting resilience and the ability to change, pressure does not destroy them. They bend and flex with what life throws at them.

But if they are stuck in their ways (aka the past), they tend to dry out and snap in our dramatically changing world. Being *resilient* means being *flexible* and *pliable*.

As I am writing this chapter, I am playing with one of my favorite toys. Donna says I am still a child at heart. I'm holding in my hand a Slinky. I've seen some plastic ones, but this is the original metal type. You may not have one now, but I bet you used to own one. My theory is that the best toys have no batteries; they last for generations and are easy for anybody to understand. The best toys bring about creativity, and they don't cost a lot of money. I wrote a book a number of years ago called *Change Is Like a Slinky*, using the Slinky as a leadership analogy for being flexible as you become an agent for change.

The Slinky was first produced in 1945, but the story began in 1943. As World War II raged across the globe, a twenty-nine-year-old naval engineer, Richard James, was stuck at the home front testing torsion springs for use as antivibration devices in navy instruments. During an experiment, he knocked a spring he was testing to the floor, and it began to exhibit a behavior that caused his jaw to drop: it was "walking" across the room. Richard showed the spring to his wife, Betty, and asked her if she thought this strange phenomenon would make a good toy. What would your spouse say if you brought some strange idea for a new toy home? Betty said "Yes!" After searching the dictionary in search of a suitable name, she arrived at the word *Slinky*, from a Swedish word meaning "to glide."

In the summer of 1945, when the war was over, Richard found a machine shop in Philadelphia that could manufacture his new toy. When the Slinky debuted at Gimbels Department Store in Philadelphia in 1946, Betty and Richard were nervous and skeptical about how well their creation would sell. In fact, they badgered some of their friends to walk up and buy some Slinkys so people would think, "Oh yeah, we really should buy this thing." They didn't need to worry. Within ninety minutes, all four hundred Slinkys for sale were purchased. The Slinky was a hit by the 1946 American Toy Fair. Since then, over 300 million Slinkys have sold worldwide, and Richard and Betty James became wealthy people. In 2015, the company celebrated seventy years of making kids and adults happy.[1]

The Slinky oozes resilience. What I like about the Slinky is how many things you can do with it. As a kid, one of my favorite things to do with a Slinky was to send it down the stairs at our house. We had wooden stairs to the basement that provided the perfect proving ground for my Slinky escapades. The Slinky is noisy and chaotic, just like change. It's unpredictable, and when you send that Slinky down the stairs, you don't know exactly where the journey will end.

Leading people in the journey of change is a lot like a Slinky. Can you live with ambiguity as you lead your team, or do you tilt toward being a control freak? Today's effective leaders learn to be resilient agents of change.

Today's effective leaders learn to be resilient agents of change.

CHANGE IS THE ONLY CONSTANT

Let me tell you about a local church that avoided resilience, to its peril. This church, very dear to my heart, followed the pattern of many others I have watched over the decades. So vibrant and relevant in the 1970s and 1980s, it became all but a sad shell of its former self. The leadership of this local church—the pastoral team and elders—asked me to come in and do a one-day workshop on change. The elders, consisting mostly of engineers, were the perfect group to start the church in the 1970s in a high-tech town. They engineered great growth and soon had over a thousand members. But as the decades passed, they continued to hold on tightly to the "old way as the only way." Sadly, they confused theology with methodology, thinking that they had to hold on to their old programs as the only right way. Engineers tend to be inflexible once they have engineered solutions to a problem. Their great strength can become an insurmountable weakness. Today, the church has dwindled to fewer than one hundred members, with few children in sight.

I was excited when the leaders brought me in to help this church. The elders asked me to advise them and answer the question "Why are all the young families in our community going to the churches down the street?" I tried to tell them, carefully and diplomatically, that they had to change. Wow, you would think *change* is a four-letter word. They did not accept my assessment. They actually said to me, "We are faithfully doing what we have always done, and if people don't come, that is their problem." To be honest, half the leaders agreed with me and half did not. They remained in gridlock and did nothing about my suggestions, because they could not agree. No decision was for sure a decision to continue their slide toward death. Their stubborn adherence to the status quo killed the church. They made the deadly mistake of clinging to the past as some sort of sacred better world.

The "R" in LEADERSHIP stands for *resilience*. Resilience means you are pliable, flexible, able to bend—like a healthy cherry tree. Every new leader must develop the practice of becoming resilient. After those elders turned a blind eye to my advice, I wanted to tell them to just "stop

Stop being so inflexible. Stop hanging on to the past.

it!" Stop being so inflexible. Stop hanging on to the past. These leaders lacked the life-giving resilience that would have served them well in revitalizing their dying church. A living tree bends with the winds; a dead tree snaps. The only constant in leadership is change. They didn't understand that you can change *programs* but still keep your *principles* intact. I was not asking them to change their timeless message—just their methods for delivering the message to their community. Their fear of losing the past paralyzed them in dealing with the future. Writer Eric Hoffer had this to say about times of change (which is all the time): "In times of change, learners inherit the earth, while the learned find themselves beautifully equipped to deal with a world that no longer exists."

You might be thinking, "Well, Hans, isn't *resilience* just another word for determination? We covered determination in chapter four. Why is resilience so important, and how can we learn to bend and not break?" Here's some great input I got from one of my podcast listeners, Tim, who is based in Southeast Asia: "New leaders tend to want to make the wholesale change immediately. This is a mistake as it usually produces too much negative sentiment and pushback. Better to wait and bring about change through deliberate and consistent vision casting for the new thing(s) and by serving one's people in order to hopefully soften their hearts and minds to the new thing(s)."[2] I like that—*soften their hearts and minds to the new things*. Resilience means being soft in spirit, not rigid, like a sapling that is healthy, flexible, and alive no matter how powerfully the wind blows. A leader who displays resilience is *not* being spineless—she *is* being responsive to the changing world in which we have to lead our team.

> Resilience means being soft in spirit, not rigid, like a sapling that is healthy, flexible, and alive no matter how powerfully the wind blows.

SHOULD I DEVELOP A THICK SKIN?

During World War II, the Germans waged war in the Atlantic Ocean with one of their most potent weapons: U-boats. These submarines were sleek black underwater vessels of destruction.

U-boats wreaked havoc, constantly harassing the shipping lanes as Allied forces moved supplies from the United States to Europe. So what did the Allies do in response? They began to destroy these U-boats with depth charges that were set to explode at a certain depth. They would pummel the U-boats for days on end, shaking up the German soldiers inside like gravel in a cement mixer.

Can you imagine being in one of those submarines and hoping to survive the explosions? It reminds me of the kind of thing that happens to us in leadership. Before we know it, we are tossed around by all kinds of forces that want to take us out. At times, leadership is a battle for survival. If you haven't experienced that yet, stay tuned! It's coming.

How do we survive the rough-and-tumble of leadership? By developing a thick skin? No. In fact, developing a tough emotional hide is the worst thing you can possibly do. Instead, work at developing a *resilient spirit*. I've had the Slinky I'm holding in my hand now for years. It's amazing; it's very hard to destroy, because it is so flexible. We need to develop that same kind of flexibility to become resilient leaders.

I've seen leaders become so well insulated and isolated that they are completely out of touch and ineffective. The church leadership team I sat with on that Saturday had circled the wagons and were in complete denial about their surroundings. Rather than develop a thick, obstinate hide as they did, we should work to develop a resilient hide, a flexible skin, that can absorb the blows, not deflect them. Instead of developing ways of never feeling the heat of leadership and never getting anywhere near a depth charge, learn how to process your surroundings with a view to the future. Your team needs you to lead out front, not hide at the rear.

RESILIENCE IS DIFFERENT FROM PERSISTENCE

In chapter four, we talked about determination, which is another word for persistence. The point we made there is that you need determination to face the depth charges that may be attacking you or your team. But in this chapter, we're emphasizing something very different. Determination alone is not enough. You need to add resilience, the ability to become strong, healthy, and successful again after something bad happens—the ability to bend in the wind and not snap; to be flexible like a Slinky.

What exactly is the difference between *resilience* and *persistence*? I want to thank my good friend David Beavers for some of these thoughts on resilience. David and I went to grad school together in the 1970s. He has successfully faced his share of depth charges, which is why he knows what he is talking about. He says resilience is actually more critical than persistence. As David has written:

> Resilience is actually more critical than persistence.

Persistence is the ability to stay in the game, to not quit, to hang in there. It's the attitude needed for the long haul—the recognition that success in our business is not a hundred-yard dash, but a marathon. Resilience is about our capacity to bounce back from difficulties, disappointments, heartbreak and hard times. My sense is that we can have persistence, but may be lacking in resilience. Resilience is critical in our business and in our lives. Persistence keeps us in the race, but resilience returns us to the right path when we get knocked off course, even knocked to the ground.[3]

In Brené Brown's bestseller *The Gifts of Imperfection,* she talks about the fact that we all want to be perfect, or we think we need to be perfect, or people expect us to be perfect. But, Brown argues, imperfection is actually a gift, and she has much to say on the concept of resilience. Brown lists the five most common factors of resilient people, based on current research:

1. They are resourceful and have good problem-solving skills.
2. They are more likely to seek help.
3. They hold the belief that they can do something that will help them to manage their feelings and to cope.
4. They have social support available to them.
5. They are connected with others, such as family or friends.[4]

Honestly, it seems to me that resilient people are the best kind of people to hang out with. They tend to be gracious and full of mercy, knowing that we are all imperfect and don't need to be treated with harsh rigidity. Understanding the gifts of imperfection helps us treat others the way we wish to be treated—with grace.

I miss that old cherry tree in our front yard. But it was rigid, and its days were numbered. The good news is that we turned that sadness into a new joy. On their fifth birthday, our twin grandchildren helped us choose a new tree in its place, a young, healthy crab apple. We are watching it grow together and celebrating this new beginning. It has already survived one major Colorado hailstorm that stripped off all its leaves. That little tree is the essence of resilience. Sometimes old things have to die before new things can take root. Change is like that. Resilience is absolutely critical for health, life, and success at home, in the family, at work, and, of course, in leadership.

Phillips Brooks was one of America's great preachers in the mid-1800s. He established schools, authored books, composed hymns, and in 1868 he published the Christmas carol "O Little Town of Bethlehem." Though our world is so very different today, this prayer Brooks wrote over 150 years ago can inspire us to pursue our dreams and to build our leadership teams with humility, integrity, and resilience:

Do not pray for easy lives. Pray to be stronger people. Do not pray for tasks equal to your powers; pray for powers equal to your tasks. Then the doing of your work shall be no miracle, but you shall be a miracle. Every day you shall wonder at yourself, at the richness of life which has come in you by the grace of God.[5]

ACTION STEPS AND DISCUSSION QUESTIONS

1. Compare yourself and your team with a Slinky. Just for fun, and for a great teaching moment, get a Slinky and have a brainstorming session with your team. Come up with a list of how many ways the Slinky applies to your team. Are you exhibiting resilience? In what areas in your business/ministry do you tend to resist change? What characteristics of leaders make them flexible and able to adapt to a changing world?

2. Listen to "Bouncing Back," my podcast interview with David Beavers. A little while ago, I interviewed David Beavers on my podcast. It would be a great interview to listen to and share with your team. Find it at www.hansfinzel.com/19.

3. Sort out your absolute team principles from your relative programs. I realize there are things that are absolutely black or white, right or wrong. These should never change. But, when it comes to methodology and strategy, we need to be resilient and open to change. If you are in ministry, you should sort out what is methodology and what is theology. Many people get tripped up, like that church I told you about, making their methodology their theology. As a team, discuss which of your team values and principles should never change. Then make a list of methods and programs that are up for grabs as the world around you changes. Pay phones and cell phones are great examples of changing communication methodology. Likewise, computers and typewriters are both methods of writing, but typewriters have become obsolete. The constant in both examples is that you need to be able to communicate; the variable is how you do it.

4. Listen to my "Do Leaders Need Thick Skin?" podcast. Many people think you need to develop a thick skin to be a good leader. I disagree. In this podcast, I tell you why this is not a good plan and how you can instead develop a resilient skin. You can find that podcast at www.hansfinzel.com/61.

"S" IS FOR SERVANT ATTITUDE

Let me tell you an amazing story about the car that love bought. Dave has been a good friend of mine here in Colorado for almost two decades. He has been the CEO of his ministry organization for twenty-five years. I consider him to be a true servant leader. Ironically, our friendship began because he wanted me to mentor him in leadership, since I am a decade ahead of him in age. As the years have gone on, I am not sure who really mentored whom. When it comes to being a true servant leader, I have learned a lot from Dave. He really lives out what a servant leader is all about.

Recently, at a gathering of Dave's entire global staff, they presented him with a check for over $11,000 to buy a car—not a brand-new car, but a car new to him. He was overwhelmed when he thanked his team. He said in a newsletter to the whole staff, "'The car that love bought'—one of my friends coined this phrase as he was coaching me in the purchasing process of my 'new' car. This is an apt description, and I want to thank you for your part in this special gift."[1]

Dave had been driving around in a dumpy old Volkswagen all the years that I'd known him. Every time we met for coffee at Starbucks, there he was in that 1996 VW. As for me, I'm a car guy. I've always loved having cool cars. In the eighteen years I have hung out with Dave, I think I went through four cars to his one VW. It's not that Dave isn't a car guy; he just didn't want to spend the money, so he drove this humble car all those years. As Donna and I did, he and his wife raised four children, and they placed other financial priorities above nice cars.

Dave went on to say in his newsletter to his staff,

> I was blown away, utterly shocked, and *completely* surprised at the conference when I was presented with the oversized card with the oversized gift of love of $11,630 designated for me to replace my worn out 1996 VW Cabrio. I'm so grateful for this expression of love....
>
> I cried tears of joy when I received this gift at the end of the conference, and I again shed tears of joy when I recently drove away from the sales transaction for my 2001 Mercedes Benz 320 roadster, hard top convertible. I have never in my life dreamed I could own such a beautiful and fun car.[2]

I recently had a chance to drive his new goldenrod Mercedes with the top down. It's beautiful. The thing that impressed me so much is that, after twenty-five years of his leadership, his staff still has such respect for him. A lot of leaders wear out their welcomes as the years march on. Dave's team knows that he has a true servant spirit and does not enrich himself as a leader, but serves those he leads instead. That's why they were thrilled to give him that car. He deserves it. What a great example of a servant leader.

SERVANT LEADERSHIP DEFINED

Everyone seems to be throwing around the phrase "servant leader." I think many misunderstand it. Some people think they are servant leaders but are far from it. "Frankly, placing *servant* in front of *leader* sounds very spiritual but seems not to have done much good," says Duane Elmer in *Cross-Cultural Servanthood*.[3]

You might wonder who first coined the term *servant leader*. As best I can tell, it originated in the 1970s. Robert Greenleaf used the phrase "servant leadership" in his 1970 essay "The Servant as Leader." Greenleaf wrote, "The servant-leader is *servant first*.... It begins with the natural feeling that one wants to serve, to serve *first*. Then conscious choice brings one to aspire to lead. That person is sharply different from one who is *leader first*, perhaps because of the need to assuage an unusual power drive or to acquire material possessions.... The *leader-first* and the *servant-first* are two extreme types."[4]

Jesus Christ demonstrated what servant leadership truly is. If you follow His life as described in the Gospels in the New Testament, you will see clearly that He walked in a spirit of humility. Certainly, He was all about being *servant first*. Humility is at the core of servant leadership.

> Humility is at the core of servant leadership.

During the final evening He shared with his team, Jesus gave His twelve disciples the ultimate visual aid of being a servant by washing their feet. Taking the initiative, He did what no one else around the table was willing to do. Before a meal in those days, a servant was usually present to wash everyone's feet because of the dusty roads. Since no servant was present, He took up the towel and basin and did the dirty work of serving His followers. His lesson was clear:

> When he had finished washing their feet, he put on his clothes and returned to his place. "Do you understand what I have done for you?" he asked them. "You call me 'Teacher' and 'Lord,' and rightly so, for that is what I am. Now that I, your Lord and Teacher, have washed your feet, you also should wash one another's feet. I have set you an example that you should do as I have done for you." (John 13:12–15)

I have always thought that if anyone ever had the right to be served and to lead as a dictator, it would have been Jesus.

After all, He was perfect, God in the flesh. But He practiced what Greenleaf called *servant first*. That is what He was driving home during those final hours with His team. He knew they would be tempted to grab power and become proud because they had served next to Jesus Christ Himself. What did Jesus mean when He asked us to wash each other's feet? To practice *servant first* with each other—bathed in humility.

As crazy as it might seem, during that very dinner, an argument arose among the disciples about who was the greatest (there goes that natural human spirit). They were positioning themselves for being C-level leaders on the team (C-level leaders are top leaders like CEOs, CFOs, and CIOs). Each felt that he deserved to be number two next to Jesus. Jesus's response went right to the servant leadership message:

> A dispute also arose among them as to which of them was considered to be greatest. Jesus said to them, "The kings of the Gentiles lord it over them; and those who exercise authority over them call themselves Benefactors. But you are not to be like that. *Instead, the greatest among you should be like the youngest, and the one who rules like the one who serves.* For who is greater, the one who is at the table or the one who serves? Is it not the one who is at the table? *But I am among you as one who serves.*" (Luke 22:24–27)

How is that for modeling what servant leadership really is? There is no better example for us to follow. Now it's time for me to share with you the definition of servant leadership that I came up with. At the end of this chapter, I will ask you to write your own. My definition for servant leadership is "when the leader cares more about the good of the team than his or her own enrichment."

> Servant Leadership:
>
> When the leader cares more about the good of the team than his or her own enrichment.

leader cares more about the good of the team than his or her own enrichment."

ALL I GOTTA DO IS ACT NATURALLY

The "S" in LEADERSHIP stands for *servant attitude*. We're going to unpack the true nature of servant leadership in this chapter, and I find it is a topic that can be very confusing. Some people mistake *servant leadership* for *slave leadership*. That is what Naomi was asking at the beginning of chapter three about the nature of servant leadership. It is not being a slave to every demand of your team 24-7.

As I mentioned in the introduction to this book, when it comes to leadership, doing what comes naturally can get you into real trouble. Buck Owens and the Beatles made "Act Naturally" a popular song in the 1960s. You probably were not around! But if you know the lyrics to "Act Naturally," you'll remember that it is about "the biggest fool that ever hit the big time."[5] Because we are naturally self-centered creatures, acting naturally is not the way to hit the big time in leadership.

I want to repeat the leadership axioms I mentioned in the introduction. In my thirty years of being a leader, watching leaders, and studying leadership, I have come to four profound conclusions that shape what I do:

- If you do what comes naturally, you will be a poor leader.
- People are confused about how to be a great leader because of poor role models. We lead as we were led.
- There are more bad leaders than good leaders.
- The world needs more great leaders.

People ask me all the time, "Why do you have such a passion for leadership?" The list above is the reason I do what I do. The world needs more great leaders and bosses. The leadership teams in churches and ministries certainly need improvement! My passion is to help leaders take their leadership to the next level. If I can help a good leader be a great leader, I am happy. If I can chip away at this list and turn things around with the leaders I come in contact with, I feel great fulfillment.

It is human nature to dominate others. We all are born with a bent toward looking out for good old

> We all are born with a bent toward looking out for good old number one—ourselves.

number one—ourselves. Serving those who are under our charge has to be learned as a new leader. Author Simon Sinek has said, "Leadership is not about being in charge, it is about taking care of those in your charge." General George S. Patton also said it well: "There is a great deal of talk about loyalty from bottom to the top. Loyalty from the top down is even more necessary, and much less prevalent. One of the most frequently noted characteristics of great men who have remained great is *loyalty to their subordinates.*"

WHAT SERVANT LEADERSHIP IS NOT

When I asked my podcast listeners the question about the most important traits every new leader should master, Michelle in Illinois wrote, "I believe that every good leader is able to understand the needs of others and act in order to provide that which is needful. A leader does not seek to gratify his or her own immediate desires; rather, he or she understands that *by helping others … the group as a whole is successful.…* It is the everyday people who can become some of the greatest selfless leaders of all time."[6] Well said!

Recently, I was teaching a group of young church leaders in China about servant leadership. In their culture, it is a huge challenge to have a positive view of leadership because of so many corrupt models of bad leadership. They see corruption and dictatorship as the leadership norm. I asked my students to help me make a list of false views of servant leadership. They loved the assignment and came up with the list below. I think it is accurate, because in most churches in their country, these are the expectations that church members have of the pastor. You may not be a pastor, but you, too, have a flock if you have people under you on your team. As you look over this list, does it remind you of some of the demands people have of you?

A false view of servant leadership—what it is *not*:

- You serve everyone.
- You do all the dirty work.
- You work 24-7 for the good of others.
- You are weak.
- Others take advantage of you.
- You carry the full load on your back.
- You are a doormat.
- You let others walk all over you.

These are all false conclusions about serving others. It is not the leader's job to be the personal butler for the team. I like to say, "We don't carry people on our backs; we carry them in our hearts." There is a big difference. And the difference is about valuing others as being as important as we are. We might be the leader or the boss, but that does not make us more valuable.

It is important to have a right view of servant leadership. You recall that we covered the issue of *accessibility* in chapter three. In that chapter I outlined some great strategies for keeping boundaries and not slipping into the tyranny of the urgent. Some followers have very unrealistic expectations of their leaders, so it is our job to teach them what true servant leadership is. I will have some tips on this at the end of the chapter.

SERVANTS ARE SHEPHERDS

The former CEO of British Petroleum, Tony Hayward, became a PR nightmare for his company during the Gulf of Mexico oil spill in 2010. In the middle of the crisis, he was quoted on international television saying, "I'd like my life back."[7] And the BP chairman, Carl-Henric Svanberg, said at the White House with cameras rolling (I could not believe he said this), "BP cares about the small people."[8]

It wasn't long before Tony Hayward had to leave his job in great humiliation—and guess what? He got his life back. You know Hayward and Svanberg probably didn't mean to condescend to the people affected by the spill—they probably meant to say that BP cares about every single person affected—but the attitude of big-time corporate executives came through as belittling the average citizen.

Donna and I were in Albania about seven years ago, speaking at a conference for church and ministry leaders in Korçë. It was thrilling to be in a country that had at one time declared itself totally atheistic. After 1990, communism died, but the church has thrived. We were blessed to be able to teach young church leaders who were trying to improve their country after so much oppression. Each afternoon after we spoke, we'd go walking up into the hills overlooking the city for exercise. Every day when we walked, we noticed a shepherd with his sheep. He never missed a day. Honestly, it didn't look like very exciting work. In fact, this shepherd seemed bored. If you think about it, it does seem like tedious work. But shepherds, good shepherds, take care of their sheep over the long haul.

Why did Jesus use the shepherd analogy for leadership? He could have used marketplace, government, or military imagery, but He chose shepherds instead. I think He used shepherds because they make a lifelong commitment to stay with their sheep. It's a life of sacrifice. Timothy Laniak interviewed shepherds all over the Middle East for his book *While Shepherds Watch Their Flocks*. In Jordan, he asked a Bedouin what it takes to be a shepherd and, sitting in front of his tent, the shepherd scratched his chin and thought for a while. Finally he said, "You know, what really matters is that you have the *heart* for it."[9]

Jesus said, "I am the good shepherd. The good shepherd lays down his life for the sheep. The hired hand is not the shepherd and does not own the sheep. So when he sees the wolf coming, he abandons the sheep and runs away. Then the wolf attacks the flock and scatters it" (John 10:11–12). It's an interesting analogy used more than any other leadership analogy in the Bible. Why do you suppose that is so? I think it is because of what I saw on those hills over Korçë. It takes real commitment and a selfless servant attitude to take care of sheep.

Leadership is not about what our people do for us; it's about what we do for our people. Leadership is

> Leadership is not about what our people do for us; it's about what we do for our people.

not about everybody serving our desires and our needs and our agendas and enriching us; it's about serving the needs of our teammates. When they're successful, we're successful. Zig Ziglar was famous for saying, "You can have everything in life you want, if you will just help enough other people get what they want."[10]

BEWARE OF THE HIRED HAND SYNDROME

So what does it look like to be a hired hand in the analogy Jesus used? How does it show up in today's world? I see it in career jumpers who move from one job to the next to further their own agendas. They're looking to go to a better opportunity, a more lucrative post. I've seen people just evaporate overnight. They're gone, and they've already taken another job. I see it when the leader is not in it for the cause or for the team. I know there are times we have to move on and take other jobs, but some leaders are nothing more than stair steppers, because they're hired hands and not really shepherds.

The shepherd says, "I want to help you fulfill your dreams"— empowerment. The hired hand says, "I'm here to pursue my dreams"—enrichment. Sooner or later, a leader has to make the conversion from *me* to *we*. *We* need to be a team, and *we* need to be successful together. When we achieve success, we all share the gains. Don't you hate it when leaders take credit for something that they didn't come up with: an idea, a program, a methodology?

Great leaders give credit where it's due, because we all share the victory together. *Leadership is not about me; it's about we.*

I came up with this chart to illustrate the contrasting viewpoints of these two kinds of leaders:

> Great leaders give credit where it's due, because we all share the victory together.

Servant Leadership—Shepherd	Self-Serving Leadership—Hired Hand
It's all about "we"	It's all about "me"
I serve others	Others serve me
I am happy if the team scores	I'm happy when I score
I carry everyone in my heart	I ride on the shoulders of everyone else
The needs of others come first	My needs come first
I am here for our cause	I'm here for my career
I am a shepherd	I am a hired hand
I want to help you fulfill your dreams	I am here to pursue my dreams
Team empowerment	Personal enrichment
We share the credit for wins	I take the credit for wins

If you look over the chart, you can see that on the right side is the leader who acts *leader first*. It is about *me*, not about *we*. The shepherd leader has the opposite attitude and game plan. His plan is to help team members be successful. Then everyone wins, and followers learn to trust their leaders—and they know that the leader is in it for the good of the team.

"LEVEL 5" LEADERSHIP

Some of you reading these pages are not in ministry but out there in the professional world. You might own a business, teach, or practice medicine. I have readers in the military and law enforcement. "Does all this servant leadership stuff work in the real world?" you might be asking.

I recall years ago speaking to a group of CEOs at a gathering in one of those tall glass buildings in downtown Chicago. They all wore their power suits and came to listen to me speak on leadership. I unpacked this theme of servant leadership, and they just didn't get it. To say the least, they were not picking up what I was laying down! They told me that to show any sign of weakness was death to their careers. I used the example of Jesus, who embodied strength bathed in service to others, but unfortunately, I don't think the concept sank in. I realized that I had not expressed servant leadership in the right terms, and they were not grasping it.

I am so thankful I found Jim Collins's amazing book *Good to Great*. That book has given me the perfect ammunition to use when speaking with high-powered leaders who have trouble with the idea of servant leadership. I love the fact that even leaders in the marketplace are getting this. It's nice to have confirmation from top leaders "out there." Jim Collins is a bestselling author and expert on leadership research. His books are based on surveys of thousands of companies. In *How the Mighty Fall*, he showed that the lack of humility is one of the major causes of corporate failures. In his classic book *Good to Great: Why Some Companies Make the Leap ... and Others Don't*, Collins described the power of servant leadership. Collins and his researchers began their quest to identify great companies by sorting through a list of 1,435 companies, looking for those that made substantial improvements in their performance over time.

After analyzing hundreds of companies, Collins observed that the leaders of the most successful, long-standing, and truly great companies, those leaders who excelled the most, are "Level 5" leaders who lead through their teams. These Level 5 leaders are humble because they clearly know their own limitations. Instead of promoting their own visions, they get their teams together and pepper them with probing questions to draw new strategies out of them. In summary, Collins found that Level 5 leaders have four traits:

- Humble
- Listened and learned constantly
- Put company above personal interests
- Valued employees first[11]

There you have it: a fresh look at a topic that gets a lot of airtime—*servant leadership*. I hope this chapter has not only inspired you to be a servant leader but also warned you about what servant leadership is *not*.

ACTION STEPS AND DISCUSSION QUESTIONS

1. How would you define servant leadership in your own words? You have read what I have to say on the topic, but how would you express it in your own words? Write your definition and discuss your answer with your team. Is there clarity around the idea?

2. On a scale of one to ten, how well do you think you do in serving your team? I guess the real question is, if your team were to answer the question, how high a score would they give you for serving them? What kind of grade would they give you on a scale of one to ten, ten being the top grade? How do you objectively give yourself a score? My friend Dave, who got the car that love bought, would probably get a nine or ten from his team.

3. Touching on the topic of slave leadership, list some of the unrealistic expectations people have of you. This is about boundaries. You have to set boundaries, and I'd encourage you to make a list of what people are demanding of you that you don't think is appropriate. Remember the woman who said, "They expect me to answer texts or emails instantaneously or certainly within several minutes." Expectations can kill you.

Throughout my career, including the last leadership position I had in ministry, I would periodically bring out the job description for which the board was holding me accountable, and I would remind my team, "These are the seven responsibilities that the board has given me and that they hold me accountable for. Some of you are disappointed in me because I am not doing what you think I should be doing, but these are my marching orders from those I report to." I wanted them to know they had some expectations of me that were not realistic and were not part of the list. Whomever you're accountable to, make sure you're clear on what your responsibilities are.

4. In light of your list under number three, how could you change your leadership style to add some boundaries yet continue serving your people? Do you need a time of clarity, or do you need to spread the load more? You have to figure out how to manage these demands. If the demands are overwhelming, they will manage you. Servant leadership is an attitude of heart: that people are important and you're serving them. But you must have boundaries. So what could you do to change? What strategy could you institute to put some fences around you so that you can get your job done and still lead your people?

"H" IS FOR HANDS-OFF DELEGATION

During my first year as the new leader of our organization, I decided we would run a full-color, half-page magazine ad for a special promotion. I called in Ted, our communications director, whose department was responsible for such things, and asked him to go to work on some ideas for me to consider. He went off, charged with a new project for the boss, not knowing that I was about to cut him off at the knees with my next move. At about the same time I gave Ted this assignment, I met a brand consultant who wanted to do some work for us. His portfolio impressed me, so I told him about the ad project and asked him if they did this kind of project. "Sure, it's our specialty," he responded. I asked him to go to work on the ad, "just for ideas," and soon received a proof from him with a great concept for the ad.

Can you guess what came next? A couple of weeks went by. Ted called me into his office with great excitement to show me the ad he had come up with. He had obviously put a great deal of work into the project. He had even gone down to the local library to scan ads in magazines similar to the one we were creating the ad for. As I looked over his work, I could tell he was anxious to please his new boss. "Ted," I told him somewhat flippantly, "it's pretty good, but I have decided to go with the consultant's concept for the ad." "What consultant?" he responded in shock. "I did not know I was in a competition and that you were talking to someone else about this project!" Boy, did I blow it. Hindsight is 20/20, and I learned a lesson that day about delegation. What I did to Ted was not fair. He had not even been aware he was competing with someone else. Needless to say, the wind went right out of his sails, and he lost trust in me.

Sometimes there is a fine line between *empowering* your team and *frustrating* your team. If you try to control them too much, they feel controlled and frustrated. If you give them freedom to grow with the healthy delegation skills I unpack in this chapter, they will grow as leaders and feel empowered.

Sloppy delegation is one of the greatest sins of leadership. There seems to be no mistake a leader makes that spreads more misery to followers. In *The Top Ten Mistakes Leaders Make*, I coined the term "dirty delegation" for this problem—*dirty* as opposed to *clean* delegation that gives the authority with the responsibility without a lot of strings attached. Dirty delegation means that there are tons of strings attached, and you are constantly looking over the shoulders of your team. You have not given the authority with the responsibility. Clean delegation, on the other hand, means that you cleanly handed over the task to your team members. You are letting them do it with freedom, not micromanaging them. Dirty delegation breeds confusion, inefficiency, and discouragement; clean delegation empowers your followers.

Ted never had the authority to do this ad. I was holding the decision making in my back pocket. I should have made it clear to him that I was just look-

> Dirty delegation breeds confusion, inefficiency, and discouragement; clean delegation empowers your followers.

ing for ideas and he was not in charge of the project. Better yet, since he was my communications director, I should have given him the whole project—that is what clean, "hands-off" delegation is all about. Strive to be known as a leader who knows how to lead well with clean delegation.

Confession is good for the soul. I have struggled with delegation over my entire career. I am not a control freak. I have the opposite problem. Let me illustrate my hang-up with the story of a couple of men who worked for me and talked about my leadership style behind my back (get used to it—all followers love to talk about their leaders). Don was an excellent chief financial officer who worked for me for a number of years. I remember the week I added a new member to my leadership team. This new person was going to be like a COO, my right-hand man. Later I heard that this new person asked Don, "What's it like to work with Hans?"

Don answered, "Well, the best thing about Hans is he gives us so much freedom to do our jobs; he does not micromanage us." "And what's the worst thing about working with Hans?" the new staff member asked. Don replied, laughing, "He gives us so much freedom." As I describe the skills of being an awesome delegator in this chapter, I will point out that leaving people entirely alone is as bad as micromanaging them.

You can't say to yourself, "Well, I'm a leader, but I never manage, so I don't need to worry about delegation." I ran across a great quote adapted from Robert Sutton's article "True Leaders Are Also Managers" in the *Harvard Business Review*, which helped me get back into balance:

> The distinction between leading and managing is a subject of ongoing debate.
>
> Leading is often characterized as the more glamorous job: leaders guide, influence, and inspire their people while managers implement ideas and get things done.
>
> But leaders who focus exclusively on coming up with big, vague ideas for others to implement can become disconnected from their team or organization. Avoid being a "big-picture only" leader.
>
> Make decisions and develop strategies that take into account the real-world constraints of cost and time. Stay involved with the details of implementation [in other words, delegate].[1]

DIRTY DELEGATION

We must be careful not to micromanage people to death. Clean delegation gives people the freedom to decide how jobs will be done. Dirty delegation confines and restricts the creativity and problem-solving potential that most people long to express. It often results in decisions made behind the backs of those to whom the work was delegated.

As I have studied delegation over the years, I have discovered four themes that occur with most leadership teams:

- Overmanaging is one of the cardinal sins of leadership.
- The lack of good delegation is rooted in fear in the leader.
- Nothing frustrates those who work for you more than sloppy delegation with too many strings attached.
- Delegation should match each worker's follow-through ability.

One of the ten essential skills every new leader must master is being a good delegator, which means being hands-off. The "H" in LEADERSHIP stands for *hands-off delegation*. Here's what we will cover in this chapter: 1) why poor delegation is so damaging in leadership, 2) four questions every follower asks, 3) how not to delegate, 4) why a lot of leaders fail miserably at delegation, and 5) ten tips for excelling at delegation.

WHY POOR DELEGATION HURTS YOUR TEAM SO MUCH

Why is poor delegation so damaging in leadership? Delegation is really an issue of how much we respect those who are under us on our team. And it is about learning to let go and developing those on our team. If we want to do everything ourselves, we will never develop a strong team of leaders under us. With responsibility comes authority to do a job. If you respect people, you'll give them the authority with the responsibility. Even if you have difficulty respecting the people you work with, you can still set a good example for them by being respectful and helping them grow in their job responsibilities.

Ronald Reagan had a little plaque on his desk in the Oval Office that read, "There is no limit to what a man can do or where he can go if he doesn't mind who gets the credit."[2] He was actually accused of being lazy because he didn't come in to the Oval Office before dawn and because in the evenings he hung out with Nancy in the private quarters of the White House. I don't think he was lazy at all—he was a master delegator. He surrounded himself with outstanding people and gave them authority with responsibility. He proved that you don't have to be a workaholic to be a great president of the United States.

I love the subject of delegation. Maybe that is why this is one of the longest chapters in the book! Here's why I love it: good delegation by you, the

> Good delegation by you, the leader, develops your people.

leader, develops your people. Delegation is really another word for *mentoring*. If you care about mentoring your team, learn to delegate well: that's what delegation will do for you. When you develop people, you mentor them, you tap into the collective genius of the team, thus building a strong team and spreading the workload.

General George Patton said, "Never tell people *how* to do things. Tell them *what* to do, and they will surprise you with their ingenuity." He was a great delegator, and he knew what it meant to empower the people he led. Here's something else he said: "If everyone is thinking alike, someone isn't thinking." I love that. It is a liability to a team when groupthink sets in and no one is allowed to contribute outside ideas that would be a big help. Patton knew that groupthink would hurt his chances of winning the battles they were fighting, because the best ideas were not being offered. Delegate—it's a powerful tool to develop the people under your charge.

FOUR QUESTIONS EVERY FOLLOWER ASKS

If you have read any of my other leadership books, you know these four questions are a common mantra for me. It's one of those things you learn in life that you refer to over and over again— simple yet profound, enduring principles of great leadership. I first heard these probably twenty-five years ago, and to this day I use the *follower questions* as one of the clearest ways to communicate delegation. The four questions every follower asks:

1. What am I supposed to do?
2. Will you let me do it?
3. Will you help me when I need it?
4. Will you let me know how I am doing?

Let's unpack these four questions. The first is, "What am I supposed to do?" This requires clear instructions and expectations. People need to know what your expectations are. Are you training them in a new skill or giving them a project that needs to get done? When I asked Ted to come up with an ad, I should have been much more clear about what he was supposed to do for me. Let's use an example: "We need a website, and here are the parameters of what we need you to do. I want you to know my expected outcomes. Here are the time and financial constraints we are under. And in terms of design, I like these examples that I have pulled off the web." It is always good to make expectations clear in terms of cost, time, concept, and decision making.

The second question every follower asks is a loaded question: "Will you let me do it?" The questions behind this question are: "Will I get the authority with the responsibility, or will you micromanage me? Will you trust me? Can I make this my own?" People want to be given responsibility; clearly tell them what needs to be done and then let them have it. This second question is really asking, "Am I going to have some freedom to put my own personality imprint into this?" People are much more motivated to do a task

> People are much more motivated to do a task if they have ownership of the project.

if they have ownership of the project. It's like the difference between renting an apartment and owning a home. Once you own a home (or a project), you pour your personality into it.

The third question every follower asks is, "Will you help me when I need it?" This is where mentoring and coaching come in. Be available as a resource, and don't be a control freak. You need to be available when they need your help, but you don't need to look over their shoulders the rest of the time. I always work hard as a leader to be there for my team when they need input, but I guard against taking the project back. When your team comes to you with a problem related to what they are working on, never say, "Oh, I'll take care of it." You just destroyed delegation and took back the authority and the responsibility. They don't want you to take it back; they just need some gentle guidance and input. Many times, I find that they just want to be assured that they are on the right track.

Finally, the fourth question is, "Will you let me know how I'm doing?" This is about feedback and check-ins; it is very important. If you work with a geographically scattered team, don't neglect this important piece of your leadership. In *The Three Signs of a Miserable Job*, Patrick Lencioni points to the problem of these last two questions not getting answered. When you are stuck in a miserable job, you feel invisible ("Nobody sees me"), you feel insignificant ("I'm not making any difference"), and you feel like an island ("I get no feedback"). Giving good feedback makes people feel they have a great job and a great boss.

> Giving good feedback makes people feel they have a great job and a great boss.

HOW NOT TO DELEGATE

I once worked with a colleague I will call Sam. Our boss, with a long lead time and very few details, gave him a huge project to tackle. We were facing some major obstacles to our work, and our leader was stumped. He knew that Sam was one smart guy, so he threw the problem at him. Being new to the team, Sam wanted to impress his boss. So he launched into the project with reckless abandon. He did tons of research, went over all kinds of solutions, and in the end delivered a fifty-page report to our boss. After a few days of not hearing anything, Sam was dying to know what the boss thought. Remember, one sign of a miserable job is "I get no feedback." There was utter silence from leadership. Finally, Sam caught up with the boss in the hallway and asked him what he thought of the proposal. The boss said in passing, "Oh, we decided to go another direction."

What did he just say?! Can you believe that? How would you feel in that situation? Sam was devastated, and he was angry—as he should have been. After that incident, Sam crawled into a sad shell of self-preservation and never regained respect for our boss. He told me bluntly with anger in his spirit, "I will never volunteer to do a project for him again." There was a huge breakdown on the part of both the leader and the follower, and in a few short years, Sam quit the team.

It is helpful to use this real-life story as a teaching moment on how not to delegate. Let's look at what the boss did wrong that really hurt Sam and disrespected him as a valuable member of the team.

As the leader, our boss did not remember what it is like to be a follower. We need to keep the thoughts and feelings of those we lead in mind. Our leader had actually never led a big team before. This was his first time, and he was clueless about how to delegate well. If you are new to leadership, please learn to delegate well. You will empower your team as they follow you. Remember what it was like when you were treated with respect.

The leader failed to give the work to Sam, to truly delegate it. There was no clarity around the questions "What am I supposed to do?" and "Will you let me do it?" If he had done this, he would not have made a decision without Sam as part of the equation. Assignments need to be given with the authority and freedom to complete the task. In the mind of Sam's boss, there never was any delegation—he was just casually looking for input. This was the same kind of thing I did to my communications director Ted with that ad project.

The leader failed to stay in touch. Without check-in points along the way of the project, there was no way for the boss to know that Sam was going all-out on this project. Honestly, I think the boss forgot in a few weeks that he had even talked to Sam about it. Sam should have demanded regular check-ins. The leader should have insisted on regular check-ins along the way as well. Don't do the entire job from start to finish and then present it to your boss gift-wrapped with a nice bow on top. You've got to have feedback along the way. That's why it's important to ask that key follower question, "Will you let me know how I'm doing?" You remember what Don, my CFO, told the new guy? "Hans tends to give too much freedom." I struggle with trusting people too much to work on their own, but I have learned that I have to stay tuned in to my team.

The boss short-circuited the decision-making process. Sam was actually never considered part of the decision-making process; the boss just wanted his opinion. Our boss should have been clear on how the decision was going to be made and how much Sam was expected to put into the project. A casual opinion would have taken a lot less time to prepare. When you delegate an assignment to someone, let her know who is going to make the final decision and where the authority lies.

The boss was playing the "inner circle game." Leaders often have a small inner circle of people whom they trust to make all the decisions. Anyone outside that circle has no authority to make decisions. I have watched two of my sons work in companies where that was the common practice. In both cases, my sons left because they had no job ownership. The top boss/ owner and his inner circle made all the decisions. Everyone else in the company was powerless. Rather than including a greater part of the organization, they kept things tight in their inner circle. People like Sam might be asked for *opinions*, but not for *decisions*. This alienates the rest of the organization and keeps the team from sharing in responsibility and decision making. It is the leadership mistake I call *dictatorship in decision making*.

WHY A LOT OF LEADERS FAIL MISERABLY AT DELEGATION

Even Moses failed at delegation in the early years of his leadership. You recall that we talked about Jethro and Moses in chapter one. In that chapter, I was underscoring that Moses learned to listen to others and changed his behavior. Now I want to illustrate that the problem he was dealing with was *lack of delegation*.

Moses was the kind of leader who thought he had to do everything himself. If Moses had kept working the way he had been, he would have eventually crashed and burned. He was already neglecting his wife and children. Jethro taught his son-in-law about good delegation. Jethro's solution to Moses's problem of too much work: spread the load! Jethro told Moses, "What you are doing is not good. You and these people who come to you will only wear yourselves out. The work is too heavy for you; you cannot handle it alone" (Exod. 18:17–18). Jethro's delegation solution:

> Listen now to me and I will give you some advice, and may God be with you. You must be the people's representative before God and bring their disputes to him. Teach them his decrees and

Jethro's solution to Moses's problem of too much work: spread the load!

instructions, and show them the way they are to
live and how they are to behave. But select capa-
ble men from all the people—men who fear God,
trustworthy men who hate dishonest gain—and
appoint them as officials over thousands, hundreds, fifties and tens. Have them serve as judges
for the people at all times, but have them bring
every difficult case to you; the simple cases they
can decide themselves. That will make your load
lighter, because they will share it with you. If you
do this and God so commands, you will be able
to stand the strain, and all these people will go
home satisfied. (Exod. 18:19–23).

Do you get that great wisdom? It was a win-win—Moses could
take a breather and focus on his tasks, and the people would actually
be happier. In addition, Moses got his wife and children back. Jethro
brought clear insight to the
problem that plagues so
many leaders: the plague of
false indispensability. "Only
I can do the job," some leaders think. But honestly, no

> The more decisions I can push downstream, the more empowered people feel and the more satisfied they become in their work.

one likes working under control freaks. The boss gets overworked,
and the workers aren't happy. I have seen in my own leadership that
the more decisions I can push downstream, the more empowered
people feel and the more satisfied they become in their work.

If you have people reporting to you, what kind of report card would they give you? On a scale of one to ten, how good a delegator are you, really? I don't think good delegation comes naturally; you have to learn it. If you struggle with delegation, you are not alone. As I have observed leaders over the years, I have figured out seven reasons why it is hard to delegate well. As you look over this list, think about what might be true of you.

- Fear of losing authority—"I will lose my power over things."
- Fear of work being done poorly—"I can do it better myself."
- Fear of work being done better—"They might show me up."
- Unwillingness to take the necessary time—"It takes a lot of time to delegate. I am in a hurry."
- Fear of depending on others—"I have this hang-up about depending on others."
- Lack of leadership training and positive delegation experience—"I have never seen it done right."
- Fear of losing value in the organization—"If they do all the work, what value am I?"

I think that every one of us leaders has at least some of these hang-ups. I have struggled with them in my journey leading others and growing a team. Growing and learning how to get past these barriers is essential for improving your delegation, which is key to growing as a leader.

Theodore Roosevelt said, "The best executive is the one who has the sense enough to pick good men [and women] to do what he wants done, and self-restraint enough to keep from meddling with them while they do it." Growing and learning how to get past your hang-ups is essential for improving your delegation skills, which is key to being a growing leader.

TEN GREAT TIPS ON AWESOME DELEGATION

When I say be "hands-off" as a good delegator, I think you understand now that I do not mean "completely out of sight." John Ortberg said, "I don't have a problem with delegation. I love to delegate. I am either lazy enough, or busy enough, or trusting enough, or congenial enough, that the notion [of] leaving tasks in someone else's lap doesn't just sound wise to me, it sounds attractive."[3] Finally, let me lay out ten positive tips on how to do this right.

1. Have a vision to develop people on your team. Delegation is a great tool for mentoring and growing your team. You can start with small assignments and then increase them as your people mature. Delegation changes people. Follow the Luke 16:10 principle: "Whoever can be trusted with very little can also be trusted with much, and whoever is dishonest with very little will also be dishonest with much."

2. Exhibit confidence in them and their work. This will grow with time as their work gets better. Have faith in them. Give them a good pat on the back when they do a good job. People love feedback, and it has been proven that work gets better with consistent positive reinforcement. If it doesn't get better, you might need to find somebody else. Some of you work with volunteers or members of your team whom you did not actually choose. In cases like that, move with the movers and ignore as much as possible those who do not show promise.

3. Make their duties or assignment clear. Be clear about your expectations so they don't go off track. This is not being controlling but being clear about what you are looking for with the assignment. I talked earlier in this chapter about the problems I had with Ted on my own team and the sour experience of my colleague Sam. In both cases there was no clarity about the task to be performed.

4. Delegate the proper authority with the responsibility. The person delegated the job should have ownership of the job. Think about the task like owning a home. You don't want them to treat it like they are just renters; you want them to exhibit pride of ownership. Be clear on who owns the task and who will make the final decision about results.

5. Don't tell them exactly how to do the work. Unless you're building an airliner or teaching them how to do brain surgery, don't tell them how to do the actual work. The basic rule of thumb is when a person is delegated a job to do, they should be allowed to choose how to do the job as much as possible. It's okay to check on their work, but we should avoid looking over their shoulder constantly, trying to make sure that they do it the way we would do it.

6. Let go of your desire to do it better yourself. The world doesn't have to revolve around the way you do things. Learn to be comfortable in your own skin, and avoid being that control freak who has to have it done his way. You might just find that your teammates can do things better than you! I learned this time and again with the team I had the joy of leading. *The sum total of all our brains and gifts is a powerful force if unleashed.*

7. Set up accountability points along the way. You remember my story about Sam who turned in the fifty-page paper only to have it tossed out? Check-in points along the way keep everyone working well together. The important thing in good delegation is that the job gets done and that the person to whom it was delegated does not go too far afield. That is why you let them know how they're doing along the way with checkpoints. During those check-in sessions, you can correct the trajectory of the project if it is going astray.

8. Supervise them according to their follow-through style. Some people need more supervision than others. I have found that some of the people who work for me run on autopilot while others need constant attention. When you work with people, you soon recognize which people are high-maintenance and which are low-maintenance. You have to adjust your style of supervision according to their personalities and their wiring. Some people need more check-in points and personal contact than others. You might want to check out the four styles of followers and how to lead them in *The Situational Leader* by Paul Hersey.

9. Give them room to fail occasionally. Did you hear the story about the brand-new IBM executive who made a million-dollar mistake? He came crawling into his boss's office knowing he was going to be fired. But the boss responded, "Fired? I just spent a million dollars teaching you a huge, valuable lesson; we're not going to fire you." You probably won't spend that much money training your team, but the lesson is clear: give them room to fail occasionally. Remember the message of Brené Brown in *The Gifts of Imperfection*: no one is perfect. The sooner we quit pretending to be, the better. Brown says that we are led to believe that if we could only *look perfect* and *lead perfect lives*, we'd no longer feel inadequate.[4] Since I cannot be perfect, how can I expect my team to be?

10. Give praise and credit for work well done. The final step of great delegation is the feedback loop. Remember, part of Patrick Lencioni's description of a miserable job is "no feedback." If the task was not done well, don't be insincere and give false feedback. But when it is done well, give them a pat on the back and tell them, specifically, how they did well. That's one of the greatest ways to develop future leaders.

ACTION STEPS AND DISCUSSION QUESTIONS

1. Try a role-play experiment in delegation. In a team discussion, walk through a typical project assignment and role-play how it would unfold. Someone take the role of the leader and another the follower. Go through the task of giving an assignment, having check-in meetings, and completing the assignment. Discuss how to master awesome delegation using the ten points I have shared in this chapter.

2. Listen to my podcasts "How to Be an Awesome Delegator— Part 1" and "How to Be an Awesome Delegator—Part 2." They're at www.hansfinzel.com/39 and www.hansfinzel.com/40. You will hear some of the ideas from this chapter and a whole lot more.

3. Review and discuss the list of the reasons why people don't delegate well. Which of these things do you struggle with? What do you feel you do well? Ask your team to give you feedback on the same questions, pointing out where you excel and what you could improve on.

"I" IS FOR INTEGRITY

Why did the Titanic sink? Prior to 1997, there was "a persistent theory ... that the iceberg tore open a 300-foot gash in the side of the 900-foot-long luxury liner." However, "an international team of scientists and engineers ... found the damage to be astonishingly small—a series of six thin openings across the Titanic's starboard hull. The total area of the damage appears to be about 12 to 13 square feet, or less than the area of two sidewalk squares."[1] It only took small gashes to sink the great ship, and it only takes small gashes to wreck a person's integrity.

Nicole was in the right place at the right time. She got into the business early and was able to build a good-sized team to work with her. Attractive, smart, and highly gifted, Nicole was a rising star in her industry. Her paycheck was growing, and she was seeing great success. But then she was tempted to take some shortcuts because she saw ways to make more money faster. Bills were piling up at home, and her husband had lost his job. With subtle opportunities to cut corners presenting themselves to her, she found herself at the crossroads of an integrity gut check. Unfortunately, she chose to cut those corners with secret decisions and actions that would be considered unethical by the company. "No one will really find out," she rationalized to herself, "and this will put me way ahead. Those rules are silly anyway, and I don't agree with them." Like many people who follow this line of decision making, she did find great success for another couple of years. Nicole's compromises, small early on, grew bigger and easier to make as time rolled on. Bills were getting paid, but she was putting small gashes in the hull of her integrity.

You can fool some of the people some of the time, but you can't fool those closest to you for very long. Nicole was eventually caught in her web of deceit and lost her business. People began to notice inconsistencies in her actions and words. Her team lost all respect for her, and sadly, it took them quite some time to recover and learn to trust leaders again. Nicole realized too late that it really was not necessary for her to cut those corners. She would have achieved great success playing by the rules—but impatience got the best of her. She was taken out not by giant gashes in her character but by tiny slits that eventually sank her promising business.

WHY DO PEOPLE FOLLOW LEADERS ANYWAY?

The "I" in LEADERSHIP stands for *integrity*. When we lose our integrity, we lose all credibility. People may still follow us because they have to, but it's not a pretty picture. Integrity is about being complete and whole. It means that you are on the inside what you claim to be on the outside. You are not a poser who pretends to be something you are not. Integrity is about honesty, ethics, and being fair. I have known people who had to work for a boss whom they knew was dishonest, and it was miserable indeed. If you find yourself in that situation, I assume you are looking elsewhere so that you can jump ship as soon as possible.

Warren Buffett, CEO of Berkshire Hathaway and one of the richest men in the world, said of integrity, "In looking for people to hire, you look for three qualities: integrity, intelligence, and energy. And if they don't have the first, the other two will kill you." I would say he has a pretty good lifetime achievement record worth copying.

> Integrity means that you are on the inside what you claim to be on the outside.

I'm going to cover three topics in this chapter related to integrity: 1) God is watching us; 2) six barriers to finishing well, no matter what your age or where you are in your career; and 3) what it means to have integrity in several essential areas of your life as a leader.

People follow leaders for all kinds of reasons. Some follow with reluctance, and others with great respect. If you are following another leader, have you ever thought about the reasons why? Do you respect her or tolerate her? On the other side of the ledger, do you have a team of followers? Why do you want them to follow you? Maybe you are a reluctant leader who doesn't really want others looking to you! You fell into leadership because of your success, and now others are counting on you to lead them. Maybe you are reading this book to learn how to lead them more effectively.

Of all the reasons people might follow you, what means the most to you? Here are six reasons I have seen why people follow leaders. Certainly not all of them are positive.

- They follow you because you are the boss.
- They follow you because they have to.
- They follow you because you pay them really well.
- They follow you because they like where you are taking them.
- They follow you because they admire and trust you.
- They follow you because you inspire them.

Obviously, the further you go down this list, the more positive and compelling are the reasons. I assume you want to be the kind of leader people follow because you are taking them to exciting places and they respect you.

What happens when you lose integrity? That is the story of Nicole. People who liked working with her lost all respect and trust. This can happen with clients and customers overnight. As I am writing this chapter, Volkswagen is in the middle of a huge scandal. It turns out this company's engineers, those supersmart Germans, figured out a software workaround in eleven million of their diesel engines that allowed them to pass emissions tests when they shouldn't have.[2] Someone was trying to cut corners to sell more cars. Many heads have already rolled in the leadership of Volkswagen. It was a great company, and it's been the world's biggest automaker. However, they have a huge problem with integrity, and it's going to take a long time to get the bad-reputation monkey off their back. By the time you read these words, they will have spent at least two years building back the reputation they lost with giant gashes in their integrity.

It takes a long time to build a great reputation but only moments to destroy it. I remember years ago we had a SWOT analysis of our ministry organization; SWOT stands for *strengths, weaknesses, opportunities, and threats.* We had seven strengths and twenty-eight weaknesses. At the end of that SWOT analysis, I was very discouraged by all the

> It takes a long time to bulid a great reputation but only moments to destroy it.

weaknesses. After watching the consultant's PowerPoint presentation, I went home totally defeated. How would we ever be able to fix our weaknesses? But the next morning, our consultant said to me, "Hans, one of your seven strengths is *organizational integrity*, and you can't buy that if you don't have it. Your donors believe in what you are doing and trust you with millions of dollars of their money." He went on to say, "Your strengths are legendary," which made me feel better about the SWOT process.

Instead of being discouraged, I should have rejoiced that we were doing well in the most important areas of our organization.

Integrity is an essential ingredient for leadership. And integrity applies not only to individuals but also to companies and organizations.

> Integrity applies not only to individuals but also to companies and organizations.

GOD IS WATCHING US— CAN THIS BE GOOD?

In 2010 Mark Hurd lost his job as the star turnaround CEO at Hewlett-Packard in Silicon Valley, California. By the time you read this, Hurd will be long forgotten and out of the headlines. HP ousted him for submitting inaccurate expense reports connected to a contractor who did marketing for the company. While investigating the contract worker's claim that Hurd sexually harassed her, HP said it discovered Hurd falsified expenses connected to her. HP's general counsel reported that in numerous instances, the contractor received compensation where there was not a legitimate business purpose.

Money and the opposite sex is an integrity issue that has taken out many a leader. Five years of brilliant leadership came to an end for Mark Hurd because of an indiscretion in his expense account, even though no illicit sexual behavior was ever confessed or discovered. Hurd claimed that someone else had messed up his expense reports. When it came to integrity, apparently he was passing the buck. He was not sweating the small stuff. What disheartens me is the way the rest of the story played out. Hurd received a $28 million golden parachute.[3] Great reward for messing up, isn't it? Most people I know who have fallen from leadership in disgrace had no parachute at all. And it is a long climb back up that mountain of your reputation.

You probably know some of the lines of the song "From a Distance" made famous by Bette Midler:

> *God is watching us*
> *From a distance*
> *God is watching us.*[4]

Well, He is watching us. If you are a Christ follower, you believe this to be true, and it affects your integrity. In fact, He is not distant at all—He is up close and personal with us. When I was growing up, I thought the fact that God was watching me all the time was bad news. But in my adult life, after becoming a follower of Jesus Christ, I realized it's great to know that God is watching me with a loving heart. The truth that God is watching me is now an encouraging concept, not a scary one.

When I was a teenager, I would watch Billy Graham crusades on TV. I remember Ethel Waters used to sing the same song at every one of Graham's crusades: "His Eye Is on the Sparrow." She had this amazingly deep voice that boomed with emotion and touched my heart deeply every time I heard it. The lyrics go like this:

I sing because I'm happy,
I sing because I'm free,
For His eye is on the sparrow,
And I know He watches me.[5]

That expresses it so very well: it's a good thing that God is watching me. The song is based on Matthew 10:29–31, "Are not two sparrows sold for a penny? Yet not one of them will fall to the ground *outside your Father's care.* And even the very hairs of your head are all numbered. So don't be afraid; *you are worth more than many sparrows.*"

As a teenager growing up in Alabama, I thought God was like a cosmic cop, waiting for me to step out of line so He could zap me. And I had a lot of behavior worth zapping! I realized later in life that I related to God just the way I related to my earthly father. I had a distant relationship with my dad. The only time I saw him was when I stepped out of line. I can remember so many times my mother saying, "Just wait till your father gets home!" I transferred that view of my father to my attitude about God my heavenly Father—that's what we naturally do. But when I grew up and began to understand who God really is and what the Bible teaches about my relationship to Him, I realized:

- God is a loving God, not a mean God.
- God looks at me with grace and forgiveness and mercy.

- God watching me is a good thing, not a bad thing.

A GREAT EXAMPLE OF INTEGRITY FROM MOSES

So God does see the good and the bad in all of us. And the good news is that, because of Christ, the negative ledger is wiped out when it comes to eternity and our standing with Him. But we still mess up in life, and our integrity must be protected very carefully. Moses wrote Psalm 90, known as the "Prayer of Moses." In verse 8 he says, "You have set our iniquities before you, our secret sins in the light of your presence." Moses knew that God was watching him all the time, and he lived out his entire journey with amazing integrity.

One place where the integrity of Moses showed up time and again was his faithfulness to God's seemingly insignificant commands. He was known as a leader who sweated the small stuff. Over and over Scripture tells us, "Moses did as the LORD commanded him" (Num. 27:22). This phrase appears ninety-four times in the Old Testament.

It's true that the devil's in the details, and we leaders usually stumble in small acts of disobedience—not in big slashes

> It's true that the devil's in the details, and we leaders usually stumble in small acts of disobedience—not in big slashes but in tiny little cuts.

but in tiny little cuts. Moses was not only a grand, visionary leader but also a man who paid attention to small details. Much of the content of the books of Moses is about minute details of legislation, lifestyle, obedience, and building the tabernacle God told him to build.

Moses knew how important it was to play by God's rules. That's why at the very end of his life, he reminded everyone again about the details of integrity and how to be successful in God's economy. When Moses finished reciting all the words to Israel, he said this to them: "Take to heart all the words I have solemnly declared to you this day, so that you may command your children to *obey carefully all the words of this law*. They are not just idle words for you—they are your life. By them you will live long in the land you are crossing the Jordan to possess" (Deut. 32:46–47). These were great leadership words as Moses passed the baton to Joshua.

Just to be clear, this integrity message is not just for spiritual people. It's not just about the Bible and what the Bible says about integrity. Some of today's greatest leadership writers in the secular realm talk about how important it is to have character and integrity in order for people to trust and follow you.

I really like to use both *integrity* and *character* when talking about who we are as leaders. I have already defined integrity, and I would say that we often use the word *character* as in "She really is a person of great character." A good character is about your inner qualities of goodness, morality, and integrity. I would hope that we would be known as people of great character. People love to follow leaders who have a reputation for having a good character. That kind of leader can be trusted and followed with great enthusiasm.

Coach John Wooden, who led the UCLA basketball team to ten national titles in twelve years, emphasized character as the key to success with his team. He said, "Be more concerned with your character than your reputation, because your character is what you really are, while your reputation is merely what others think you are."[6]

In the introduction to the second edition of their landmark book, *Leaders: Strategies for Taking Charge*, Warren Bennis and Burt Nanus observe, "Although a lot of executives are derailed (or plateaued) for lack of character or judgment, we've never observed a premature career-ending for lack of technical competence. Ironically, what's most important in leadership can't be easily quantified."[7] These writers in the secular realm know that character is a key issue for effective lifelong leadership. In fact, they admit that the longer they study effective leaders, the more they have seen that character is the defining issue. They would agree with the hiring practices of Warren Buffett.

SIX BARRIERS TO FINISHING WELL

When you're in your twilight years, how will you describe success as you look back on your life? I think David in the Old Testament had a pretty good idea. Despite major integrity failures in his life, he finished well. Yes, God is watching us, but He is also waiting and eager to forgive us when we mess up. I take a lot of encouragement from David's story that there is hope for all of us. He said in Psalm 41:11–12, "I know that you are pleased with me, for my enemy does not triumph over me. Because of my integrity you uphold me and set me in your presence forever."

When I was working on the material for this chapter, I wrote to some friends to get their responses to this legacy question: "How would you describe a successful life when you're looking back from the finish line?" I asked leadership guru John Maxwell and was honored that he took the time to write me back. I love his answer: "I have always stated that my definition of success is that those closest to me love and respect me the most. So I will have finished well if at the end ... those closest to me, who knew me inside and out, love and respect me the most."[8] Wow, that is a great way to define integrity.

Remember the young man I mentioned in my chapter on determination, who, in his early thirties, had left a job to move to a new company after being trapped in a miserable job for almost three years. At the farewell gathering, he discovered that he had a sterling reputation with both his bosses and his team, who gave him a warm farewell, with everyone hating to see him go. Whether you are young or older, I'm talking about finishing well with integrity in your current assignment. Sadly, we know that many leaders don't finish well and don't leave well.

Dr. Bobby Clinton, who taught for many years at the Fuller School of Intercultural Studies, has studied thousands of leaders over his lifetime. He was my mentor and advisor for my doctorate in leadership. I was his teaching assistant and enjoyed a close relationship with this man from whom I learned a lot about leadership. Though he's retired now, a lot of people still look to Bobby Clinton for leadership studies and keys to finishing well. He based his *leadership emergence patterns* on what he observed in thousands of lives of leaders. He studied scores of biblical leaders and secular leaders as well as famous Christian leaders. You might want to pick up his book *The Making of a Leader: Recognizing the Lessons and Stages of Leadership Development*.

Here are Clinton's six barriers to finishing well. I have listed them here and added my own comments about each one:[9]

1. Finances. As leaders grow in influence and the amount of money they are responsible for, greed and mismanagement can easily creep in and compromise their character. Examples in the Bible would be Gideon's golden ephod and Ananias and Sapphira, who cheated the early church and lied about how much money they had given the church. Their story did *not* end well (see Acts 5:1–10). I was the CEO of a ministry with a $34 million annual budget. I was at a place where I could have abused my expense account, but I obsessed about turning in very thorough expense reports with all the proper receipts. I remember one time Christina, our financial clerk who tracked expenses and reimbursements, said, "You do a better job than anybody at turning in all the details of your expenses." I thought to myself, "Well, yeah, I think I should." We at the top, more than anybody, should be held accountable to a very high standard. Finances trip so many people up.

2. Power. With the growth of power comes the subtle temptation to abuse it. Privileges come with a rise in perceived status, which can easily be abused. We see this a lot in Washington among politicians. An example in the Bible would be Saul's usurping of priestly privilege. Abraham Lincoln said, "Nearly all men can stand adversity, but if you want to test a man's character, give him power." Power can derail you; it can get in your head. All of a sudden, you think you don't have to obey the rules, or you live by a different set of standards. Power can become absolutely addicting; it can

> Power can become absolutely addicting; it can become like a drug that changes your perception.

become like a drug that changes your perception, and suddenly you rationalize, "I am special and special rules apply to me."

3. Pride. Bobby Clinton says we must maintain a healthy respect for who we are and what we've accomplished, but we must not allow our successes to go to our heads. We should give God credit for anything good that comes out of our work. It's so important that we understand the battles of pride and how pride comes before a fall. Self-confidence is a good thing and necessary for success in leadership, but guard your heart so that your confidence does not creep over to that dangerous place of arrogance. I'm going to have a lot to say about the problem of pride in the final chapter of the book.

4. Sex. This has been a key test of leadership from day one. Joseph, in the Old Testament, did it right; David did it wrong.

Be careful of the monster of illicit sex, and maintain the correct, appropriate relationships with the opposite sex. Proverbs 4:25–27 says, "Let your eyes look straight ahead; fix your gaze directly before you. Give careful thought to the paths for your feet and be steadfast in all your ways. Do not turn to the right or the left; keep your foot from evil." This applies not only to the people you come in contact with, but also to the media you visit online. There are many good resources for any of you who struggle with this, including books, websites, and men's and women's support groups and conferences.

5. Family. Tension and trouble in the leader's home can result in his leadership being destroyed. This tension can be between a husband and a wife or between parents and children or even battles between siblings. I personally think that if you are married and have a family, they should be a huge priority for you. Workaholics tend to neglect their families to their ruin. What good does it do to gain the whole world with financial success and lose your marriage and children? No one says at the end of her life, "I wish I had spent more time at the office." No, by that time in life, we realize that what matters most is loved ones and our family. Proverbs 28:6 says, "Better the poor whose walk is blameless than the rich whose ways are perverse."

6. Plateauing. I was surprised at Bobby Clinton's final barrier to finishing well. But it makes sense. Over the years of a long-term leadership assignment, we can subtly morph from passion to paralysis. A calling we once loved and thrived in becomes routine and even boring. Things that jazzed us in our thirties weary us in our fifties. Some leaders don't burn out—they dry out. They experience a growing dullness in their work. If it's not countered with lifelong learning and renewal, plateauing will reduce the leader's effectiveness to zero. It was Bobby who first taught me the value of lifelong learning. That is why I made the "L" in LEADERSHIP stand for *listen* and *learn*!

PREDICTABLE AND SUSTAINABLE TRUST

The longer I live, the more I find that matters of the heart reign supreme in the lives of all leaders. These are the soft issues of leadership, mentioned at length in chapter two on emotional intelligence. Guard your heart carefully, and your leadership will soar.

> Above all else, guard your heart,
> for everything you do flows from it.
> (Prov. 4:23)

There's a common adage that "your gifts and skills might get you to the top, but only your character will keep you there." The third and final thing I want to cover in this chapter is more positive than the first two. After looking at the six barriers to finishing well, let's flip it around and look at a few areas that are especially critical to leaders when it comes to character. In reading the lives of great men and women, I found that the first victory they won was over themselves. Self-discipline came first with all of them. Here are some of my favorite scriptures on integrity:

> The integrity of the upright guides them, but the unfaithful are destroyed by their duplicity. (Prov. 11:3)

> The LORD detests lying lips, but he delights in people who are trustworthy. (Prov. 12:22)

> Pray for us. We are sure that we have a clear conscience and desire to live honorably in every way. (Heb. 13:18)

The other day, I was speaking to a group of high-level leaders, and I asked them, "In leadership we want to *make a mark* and we want to *leave a legacy*. What's more important to you, making a mark or leaving a legacy?" Making a mark is what you accomplish as a leader through your team, through your business, through your ministry, through your church, through your nonprofit, through your school—whatever you're doing. A leader makes things happen, great things happen. That's the joy and the payback of the work of leadership. We make a mark, but we also leave a legacy, and that's just as important—maybe more so. I think both are equally important in our career. How would you answer my question? The kind of legacy we leave is all about our reputation and integrity. I will share more about leaving a legacy in chapter ten.

PROMISES KEPT AND CONFIDENCES HELD

Reliable leaders keep their promises. That trait often separates leaders from followers. Our ministry faced a major issue that required strict confidentiality. We were relocating our offices from Chicago to Denver. For the information to leak out prematurely would have been very destructive to our employees, our families, and our personnel worldwide. I watched with interest as we on the leadership team committed to share this information only with our spouses for a period of several months. I'm proud to say that the group kept a tight lid on the information.

> Reliable leaders keep their promises.

After several months, we discovered a leak of confidentiality. When the information finally leaked, it was not through my team but from another person who was in on the secret but could not keep it to himself. You know how it works—we know a secret, and we are dying to tell someone. "Listen, I'm not supposed to say this, but if you promise you won't tell anybody, I guess I can tell you." That's not keeping a secret. That's not keeping your word. He confidentially told a good friend who was asked not to repeat it but who in turn told another friend in confidence not to repeat it—and on it went. The secret was broken. That first person in the chain really let us down.

He initiated a series of events that was hurtful. Fortunately, the damage was minimal because it was just before the time to release the information officially. Here's a lesson to learn: don't give out confidential information that's entrusted to you. Can people trust you? Knowledge is power. We're tempted to share confidential information, because knowing a secret makes us seem important.

What about your promises? When you are asked to come to an event or do something for someone else, are you honest out of the gate? James in the New Testament summed up this quality of trust-worthiness: "Above all, my brothers and sisters, do not swear—not by heaven or by earth or by anything else. All you need to say is a simple 'Yes' or 'No.' Otherwise you will be condemned" (James 5:12). In our culture, we have allowed this area to slip big-time. So many people will say yes when they have no intention of following through, because a yes is easier. A firm no can cause you to lose face. Don't say yes to something when in reality you have no inten-tion of doing it either because you have no authority or ability to do it or no desire to do it. Let your yes be yes, and let your no be no. Just try it for a while—you might be surprised how liberating it is to be a person who shoots straight with others. Use words of grace when you gently but firmly tell people no. You will be known as a person who keeps his word. Another good way to respond, and one that avoids a false yes, is to say, "I am not sure. Let me get back to you after I have considered your request."

A common proverb says, "Integrity is doing the right thing even when no one is watching." I chose *integrity* as the "I" in LEADERSHIP because it is so significant. It is not really a leadership skill, but is an essential leadership characteristic for success. If you follow the lives of great leaders, living or dead, you will find that they were the same people alone as when others were watching. That is what we strive for in leadership, and it is one of the first great goals of a new leader starting out. Establish early on the habit of making the right choices, and it will serve you well as you grow in your leadership influence.

ACTION POINTS AND DISCUSSION QUESTIONS

1. Talk about the finish line question. Discuss with your team how you would answer the legacy question, "How would you describe a successful life when you're looking back from the finish line?" Make a list of what matters most to you and what you would like said about you at your funeral.

2. Areas of integrity that tempt you the most. What areas of your character tempt you the most to make compromises? Have you already made compromises that have hurt your leadership? If so, what can you do to make changes? Should you confess to your team as part of a healing process? Is it time to confess to God and ask Him for forgiveness and help getting out of bad patterns or habits?

3. Check out my book *The Power of Passion in Leadership.* This book addresses the problem of plateauing, which I went through in my own career. If you are in a place of being stuck in a miserable job, or you are totally without passion in what you do, read *The Power of Passion in Leadership*. It's available in Kindle, paperback, and audiobook formats. In it, I talk about how to do what you love and love what you do, and why you should consider moving on if you cannot make your current job work for you.

4. Read the story of Ananias and Sapphira in Acts 5:1–10. Why do you suppose they lied to the church? Did they need to? It is interesting to note in this story that the couple had an integrity problem in their marriage, not just as individuals. They were in cahoots, to their own peril. What lessons can you learn for your own leadership from their story?

5. How do we guard our hearts? We saw this verse from the book of Proverbs: "Above all else, guard your heart, for everything you do flows from it" (4:23). What does it mean that everything we do flows from the heart? How does that apply to leadership? Can you make a list of the ways you can guard your heart in the grind of leadership? This would be a great team discussion.

6. Make a mark or leave a legacy? Discuss this question with your team. How do you see yourself making a mark in your current career? Make a list of what will satisfy you the most. When it comes to legacy, how do you want people to remember you? This circles back to the first question about your finish line.

"P" IS FOR THE POWER OF HUMILITY

Let me tell you about Max. Max was young, sharp, tall, gifted, and had a lot of charisma. Growing up, he always fell naturally into leadership. As a young adult committed to Christ, he aspired to be a leader for God. Max felt that God had endowed him with leadership ability, and he honed it through his college and postgraduate education. He graduated from a premier seminary and received his first ministry assignment: team leader for a new ministry that was born out of great vision. You might say he became the leader of a ministry start-up.

Things were going great for a while. Max was getting a lot done and even published a book in his early thirties. He was feeling great about his career and all his early success—until it all came crashing down around him one day. During the annual business meeting of the ministry team at the end of year two,

Max was "deselected" as leader by his colleagues. Someone else from his team was put in his place. He was devastated … because he really thought he was God's gift to the world, and certainly to his team. He had not seen this vote of no confidence coming. When he picked himself up off the floor and finished licking his wounds, he asked a few of his colleagues what had happened. "You don't really care about us, Max. You only care about your agenda and getting your tasks done. We want a leader who has a heart and pastors us like a shepherd."

Ouch. That hurt … badly. It was painful, and it was true. The reason I know this story so well is that it happened to me. Max is really Hans. The person I described was me as a new leader in my early thirties. My own team cast me aside and sent me to the desert to learn some painful lessons. I came to appreciate that people will never care how much you know (or do) until they know how much you care about them.

I don't know how gifted you are, but I have seen that the more you have going for yourself naturally, the more pride can get in the way of genuine success. I had to learn the same leadership lesson that Moses had to learn in Egypt after he tried to rescue his own people in his own strength. They rejected him outright: "'Who made you ruler and judge over us? Are you thinking of killing me as you killed the Egyptian?' Then Moses was afraid and thought, 'What I did must have become known'" (Exod. 2:14). He fled to the desert and, over the next forty years, God took the pride and arrogance completely out of him. D. L. Moody said of Moses, "Moses spent his first forty years thinking he was somebody. He spent his second forty years learning he was a nobody. He spent his third forty years discovering what God can do with a nobody."[1]

You can call it youthful arrogance, overconfidence, egotism, haughtiness, or just plain pride. But it affects a lot of gifted leaders just starting out. The "P" in LEADERSHIP stands for the *power of humility*. I included it because its opposite, pride, is so common in poor leaders. New leaders, like Moses, often make the mistake of leading with their natural talent, personality, gifts, and smarts. They lead with their heads, not with their hearts. In my early years in leadership, I was arrogantly full of myself, not humbly full of God. The problem of pride plagued me.

As I mentioned in the last chapter, there is a well-known saying, "Your gifts might get you to the top, but they won't keep you there." As the years have gone by and I have watched other leaders rise through the ranks, I have seen an interesting pattern. The more gifted we are, the more talented we are, the greater our education, the more tendency there is to rely on those skill sets to lead—to lead by a powerful personality and ego. Those will carry us for a while, but sooner or later, there comes a reckoning related to our arrogance. And if that reckoning does not come, neither will truly great leadership.

Have you ever worked under a domineering leader who has this ego problem? I have. In their lack of humility, they make life miserable for those under them because they are horrible listeners and tend to be control freaks. These leaders have all the answers, so why ask any questions? They act like they are better at everything than those who work for them.

Between the time Moses was forty and eighty, he had a leadership conversion. He became humble, and through that conversion, God gave him powerful leadership credibility. In fact, the Bible says that he eventually became "more humble than anyone else on the face of the earth" (Num. 12:3). I don't think I could have endured forty years of obscurity in the desert as he experienced, but he had a lot of Egyptian arrogance to get out of his system. After all, he was very gifted and was raised in Pharaoh's household.

> Humble leadership is not leader first—it is servant first.

In his youthful zeal, Moses failed as he tried to lead by his own sheer strength of position and personality. But when he was eighty, he was fully prepared to lead with strength bathed in humility. His confidence was no longer in his gifting. In fact, he told God at the burning bush that He had the wrong man. At forty, he was eager to lead; at eighty, he was a reluctant leader. As he was being summoned for the leadership challenge of a lifetime, he told God that he had no gifting: "Master, please, I don't talk well. I've never been good with words, neither before nor after you spoke to me. I stutter and stammer" (Exod. 4:10 THE MESSAGE). We know that is not true because of what is said of him in the book of Acts: "Moses was educated in all the wisdom of the Egyptians and was powerful in speech and action" (Acts 7:22).

What would this kind of leadership look like in our modern world? A leader like that would be strong yet gentle in spirit and would have passionate personal resolve clothed in a humble spirit.

Humble leaders know the value of every team member and are not full of themselves. They are passionate about what they and their team are up to. Humble leadership is not leader first—it is servant first. When you are empty of pride, you can be full of all the great attributes that inspire others to follow you.

You have heard the stories in this book about my frustration with working with prideful leaders. I have also worked under humble leaders in my career. What a delight! People love following humble leaders who lead passionately with their hearts out front for all to see. Heart-to-heart trust is built between leaders and followers. Loyalty grows in followers who respond to humble leaders who lead with a passionate shepherd's heart. That is not to say that they cannot be men and women of great gifting and ability, but they don't overpower people with their talent.

WHY SHOULD THEY FOLLOW YOU?

Bringing this list forward from the last chapter, I want to ask the question again in the context of humility. Of all the reasons people should follow you, which one means the most to you? Do you see why the lower down the list you go, the better your leadership is?

- They follow you because you are the boss.
- They follow you because they have to.
- They follow you because you pay them really well.

- They follow you because they like where you are taking them.
- They follow you because they admire and trust you.
- They follow you because you inspire them.

In my early years of leadership, my team followed me because they had to. I was stuck at the top of this list, and I don't wish that for anyone. I was their appointed leader, and the first chance they got, they voted me off the island. In hindsight, it really was the best thing that ever happened to me as a young leader. It caused me to look inside myself and learn the early valuable lessons of the *heart* and of *humility*. It is all about humble hearts, not prideful heads.

The best kind of leaders are like my friend Dave, whom I told you about in chapter seven—his team gave him a new car after twenty years of leadership because they love and respect him so much. They know that Dave has a shepherd's heart for them; it comes through with the genuine love he shows for his team. They have never seen him as just a hired hand.

Here is a simple test to see how you are doing with pride and humility in your leadership. How well do you take feedback about your leadership? Do you even look for it? Prideful leaders don't want feedback, and they get defensive if it is offered. Humble leaders know that feedback is part of healthy, mature leadership. We all have to learn to improve our game. When my team told me what was wrong with me in those early days, I was devastated. I immediately got defensive and angry with them. I tried to explain it all away and justify myself. But then one of my mentors gave me some great advice: "Look for the 5 percent of truth in what they are saying about you." Well, I did, and actually it was more like 50 percent! In my subsequent years of leadership, I have always asked for feedback and responded first with these two words: "Thank you." Starting with those two power words puts you in the right frame of mind to avoid defensiveness and learn.

You might think it strange that I would use both Moses and Steve Jobs as examples of leaders with humility. But think about it: Moses tried to help and lead the children of Israel before God had appointed him and before he was ready, and the Israelites rejected him. Just as Moses was rejected by the Israelites, Steve Jobs was fired—from the company he founded. And I thought I had problems on my little team!

> Humble leaders know that feedback is part of healthy, mature leadership. We all have to learn to improve our game.

On June 12, 2005, Steve Jobs gave the commencement address at Stanford University. His topic was "You've got to find what you love." I highly recommend you find that short speech on YouTube and listen to it. He said that his firing was the best thing that ever happened to him as a leader. It humbled him and gave him a chance to mature. He had a gut check and a heart check.

Steve Jobs was notoriously tough to work with. He had an extraordinary dose of talent and gifting. If you read his life story, you will learn that he was very demanding as a leader. But as tough as he was on people, he garnered extreme loyalty. On a recent trip to China, I saw the biggest Apple stores ever, and everyone seemed to have an iPhone and iPad. A friend in Beijing told me his young son who wants to learn English had just learned his first word: "Apple." That impact goes back to Steve's passion as a leader. He was not just pushing himself; he had a passion to change the world. Steve Jobs made a huge mark and left a great legacy. He developed a tribe of loyal followers because he was doing work he loved, not just trying to make money. He led with his heart out front. Here is a small excerpt from that Stanford commencement speech:

> Your work is going to fill a large part of your life, and the only way to be truly satisfied is to do what you believe is great work. And the only way to do great work is to love what you do. If you haven't found it yet, keep looking. Don't settle.[2]

If you love what you do and care about the people you work with, you will do fine as their leader. People get into trouble when they lead for their own egos or for what is in it for them. My mentor in graduate school, Howard Hendricks, had a great piece of advice for young leaders: "Your career is what you are paid for; your calling is what you are made for."[3] When you find that sweet spot of doing what you are made to do, you can lead with your heart out front, fully alive, and from a place of humility.

Followers are smart. They are not dumb like sheep. They know the motives of those who lead them. When I was a young leader, I have to admit, I made things all about *me*. It was my quest to be successful and make a name for myself. I guess I had a lot of pride and self-centeredness to deal with. I had to learn the conversion from *me* to *we*. I had to learn to lead with my heart out front, vulnerable, accessible, and caring about my people like a shepherd, not a hired hand. It reminds me of what the apostle Peter shared with his budding new leaders in the book of 1 Peter:

> Care for the flock that God has entrusted to you. Watch over it willingly, not grudgingly—*not for what you will get out of it*, but because you are eager to serve God. (5:2 NLT)

MAKE A MARK—LEAVE A LEGACY

Ultimately, we want to make a mark and leave a legacy as leaders. Some of us will leave bigger marks than others, but we will all leave a legacy. When we are young, our leadership is mostly about making a mark. When we get older, it seems we're more concerned about leaving a legacy. The two ideas are actually connected. *We create our legacy as we leave our mark*. Our legacy will be remembered as positive or negative by those we led. If positive, they will think of us as having a good heart and taking them to great places they could not have reached themselves. They will remember that we

> Our legacy will be remembered as positive or negative by those we led. If positive ... they will remember that we cared about the people, not just the task.

cared about the people, not just the task. On the negative side of the ledger, some leaders leave and the followers throw a party. "Yay, she is finally gone! She only looked out for her own career, and her heart was never really with us. She used the position as nothing more than a stepping-stone."

In my career, I have had three farewell milestones. I had three major positions of leadership over a span of thirty years, and in each case, they threw a farewell event for Donna and me at my departure. I remember each occasion vividly. I wonder what everyone was thinking at those gatherings. Actually, I am glad I don't know what was said in hushed whispers. Some were grateful for my legacy, and if I am honest with myself, I know that some were glad I was moving on.

What will be said about you at your farewell event? I hope when you leave your current leadership assignment, it will be on good terms. Trust me, that day will come. None of us are indispensable. Sooner or later, we move on. Leaders leave a legacy whether they plan to or not. The truth is, we rarely think about our legacy while in the daily grind of leadership. But when we do finish up, what will we have left behind in our wake? In the end, I want to be remembered for the *kind of person I was* (I want to leave a legacy) and the *difference I made* (I want to make a mark).

One of the greatest brief leadership tributes in the Bible is about King David. Here was a man mighty in gifts: he had talent, looks, personality, and strength. But look what comes through about his legacy. The thing that David knew, and that Moses learned, is that God uses leaders who rely first on God and lead with a humble heart. King David is remembered as one of the greatest leaders of God's people.

> God uses leaders who rely first on God and lead with a humble heart.

> And David shepherded them with integrity
> of heart;
> with skillful hands he led them.
> (Ps. 78:72)

I love that verse because it expresses the soft and hard skills of effective leadership. People should first and foremost remember what our hearts were all about. If people say of me at my funeral, "He had a good heart as he led others, and he loved his family," then I can go to my reward a happy man. All of us as leaders should want the kind of tribute that David received in this psalm.

COMING FULL CIRCLE BACK TO "L"

I mentioned Jim Collins in chapter seven on servant attitude. What he discovered in his research very much applies to this chapter on the power of humility. In *How the Mighty Fall*, he showed that arrogance and the lack of humility are major causes of corporate failures. In his classic book *Good to Great*, Collins recognized the power of servant leadership, calling it "Level 5" leadership. Level 5 leaders are humble because they clearly know their own limitations.[4] Instead of only promoting their own visions, they draw new strategies out of their team.

I started this book by looking at the letter "L" in LEADERSHIP. Do you recall what it stands for? It stands for *listen* and *learn*, the two most important words in the leader's vocabulary. The first and most important mistake new leaders need to avoid is lack of listening and learning. And do you see how pride gets in the way of both of these skills? If you think you have all the answers, you won't listen. If you have not dealt with your pride, you certainly won't be learning new things. From a place of humility you can be a truly great, lifelong leader who will make a significant mark and leave a lasting legacy.

Humility really is a major positive driving force in every walk of life. The power of quiet humility overcomes a world of other inadequacies you might be facing. Dostoevsky excellently summarized the importance of humility: "Loving humility is a terrible force, the most powerful of all, the like of which there is none."[5]

ACTION STEPS AND DISCUSSION QUESTIONS

1. Do you have the blessing of being highly talented and gifted? It's okay—you can admit it. I am the kind of person who can do a lot of things well, and pride is a temptation for me. Would you say you struggle with pride because you can do a lot of things well?

You might need a gut check about how you are coming across to others. Can you see how your gifts can get you into trouble in your leadership? Talk with your team about how you have dealt with this up to this point in your journey. Ask for honest feedback about how you come across. Be willing to grow.

2. Watch the Steve Jobs commencement address. On June 12, 2005, Steve Jobs gave the commencement address at Stanford University. His message was, "You've got to find what you love." Watch that short speech on YouTube and discuss it as a team. Jobs says his firing was the best thing that ever happened to him as a leader. Why did he say that? What lessons did you take away from his talk? Do you see how his experience can help you in your leadership journey?

3. Take a lesson from a domineering leader you have worked under. If you have worked under a leader filled with pride, you are not alone. Your negative experience can be highly instructive now. How did that person make you feel? What can you learn about that negative experience to make yourself a better leader? In what ways did pride manifest itself? Are you in danger of doing the same? Discuss the fallout of this kind of leadership with your team.

4. How does humility show up in your workplace? Turning the previous question around, have you worked for a leader that displayed great humility? Describe the characteristics that he or she exhibited. Does that leader speak into your life in a specific way?

5. Make a mark or leave a legacy? I hope you got the point I was making about these two outcomes of leadership. I want you to think about it as it relates to what you are doing in your career. If you are in a discussion group, talk about what these two things mean. What is more important to you right now in your leadership journey? Why? What legacy would you like to leave as people remember you? You might be young and have fifty years ahead of you, but it is never too soon to think of the legacy you are creating. Like a speedboat on a lake, we all leave a wake that makes a deep impression on others.

NOTES

INTRODUCTION

1. John Rogers, "Sentenced Official Who Became Face of Civic Corruption Leaves Huge Debt for California City," *U. S. News & World Report*, April 16, 2014, www.usnews.com/news/us/articles/2014/04/16/ex-california -city-leader-gets-12-years-in-prison.

CHAPTER ONE

1. Kohei Goshi, quoted in Duane Elmer, *Cross-Cultural Conflict: Building Relationships for Effective Ministry* (Downers Grove, IL: InterVarsity, 1993), 11.

2. Spencer Johnson, *Who Moved My Cheese? An Amazing Way to Deal with Change in Your Work and in Your Life* (New York: Putnam's Sons, 1998), 91.

3. Frances Hesselbein and Paul M. Cohen, *Leader to Leader: Enduring Insights on Leadership from the Drucker Foundation's Award-Winning Journal* (San Francisco: Jossey-Bass, 1996), 78.

CHAPTER TWO

1. Chris, quoted in "64: Learn to Lead: Ten Essential Skills Every New Leader Must Master: Emotional Intelligence," HansFinzel.com, July 29, 2015, www.hansfinzel.com/64; emphasis added.

2. Joe, quoted in "64: Learn to Lead."

3. "An intelligence quotient (IQ) is a total score derived from one of several standardized tests designed to assess human intelligence. The abbreviation

'IQ' was coined by the psychologist William Stern for the German term *Intelligenzquotient*, his term for a scoring method for intelligence tests he advocated in a 1912 book." "Intelligence Quotient," *Wikipedia*, last modified September 16, 2016, https://en.wikipedia.org/wiki/Intelligence _quotient.

4. Jordan, quoted in "64: Learn to Lead."

5. "Grow Your Emotional Intelligence," LeadershipTraQ, accessed September 20, 2016, http://leadershiptraq.com/life-tips/grow-your-emotional -intelligence/.

6. John Ortberg, *Everybody's Normal Till You Get to Know Them* (Grand Rapids, MI: Zondervan, 2014), 161.

7. "Grow Your Emotional Intelligence."

8. "About Emotional Intelligence," TalentSmart, accessed September 20, 2016, www.talentsmart.com/about/emotional-intelligence.php.

9. Henry Deneen, quoted in "31: Emotional Intelligence—An Interview with Henry Deneen," HansFinzel.com, April 17, 2014, www.hansfinzel.com /episode-31; emphasis added.

CHAPTER THREE

1. Carlo Maria Giulini, quoted in Warren Bennis and Burt Nanus, *Leaders: Strategies for Taking Charge*, 2nd ed. (New York: HarperCollins, 2003), 52.

2. Aisha Tyler, "Aisha Tyler Does It Her Way" (lecture, Omni Hotel, Fort Worth, TX, July 30, 2015).

3. "Brené Brown: How Vulnerability Can Make Our Lives Better," interview by Dan Schawbel, *Forbes*, April 21, 2013, www.forbes.com/sites/danschawbel /2013/04/21/brene-brown-how-vulnerability-can-make-our-lives-better /#5afc9ee760ba/.

4. "Being Vulnerable about Vulnerability: Q&A with Brené Brown," interview by Roxanne Hai, *TEDBlog*, March 16, 2012, http://blog.ted.com/being -vulnerable-about-vulnerability-qa-with-brene-brown/.

CHAPTER FOUR

1. Steven Pressfield, quoted in "How to Overcome the Resistance," MichaelHyatt.com, March 6, 2013, https://michaelhyatt.com/044-how-to -overcome-the-resistance-podcast.html.

2. Some of the information regarding Colonel Sanders and Nelson Mandela was adapted from my previous book coauthored with Rick Hicks, *Launch Your Encore: Finding Adventure and Purpose Later in Life* (Grand Rapids, MI: Baker, 2015), 102–3.

3. Jim Rohn, "The Two Choices We Face," GetMotivation, accessed September 20, 2016, www.getmotivation.com/jimrohn/jim-rohn-two-choices-we-Face.html.

4. Oprah Winfrey, "What I Know for Sure," Oprah.com, Feb. 2003, www.oprah.com/omagazine/What-I-Know-for-Sure-Becoming-Who-You-Are.

CHAPTER FIVE

1. Tim, quoted in "67: Learn to Lead: Ten Skills Every New Leader Must Master: Effective Communication," HansFinzel.com, October 6, 2015, www.hansfinzel.com/67.

2. Rev. Gibbs, quoted in "67: Learn to Lead."

3. Max De Pree, *Leadership Is an Art* (New York: Doubleday, 1987), 108; emphasis added.

4. Patrick Lencioni, *The Four Obsessions of an Extraordinary Executive: A Leadership Fable* (San Francisco: JosseyBass, 2000), 166.

5. Jeff Bezos, quoted by John Cook, "Full Memo: Jeff Bezos Responds to Brutal NYT Story, Says It Doesn't Represent the Amazon He Leads," *GeekWire*, August 16, 2015, www.geekwire.com/2015/full-memo-jeff-bezos-responds -to-cutting-nyt-expose-says-tolerance-for-lack-of-empathy-needs-to-be-zero/.

CHAPTER SIX

1. Portions of this adapted from my previous book, *Change Is Like a Slinky: 30 Strategies for Promoting and Surviving Change in Your Organization* (Chicago: Northfield, 2004), 59–60.

2. Tim, quoted in "68: Learn to Lead: Ten Skills Every New Leader Must Master: Resilience,"HansFinzel.com, October 7, 2015, www.hansfinzel.com/68.

3. David Beavers, "Bouncing Back," DavidBeavers.net, August 28, 2013, https://davidbeavers.net/2013/08/28/bouncing-back-3/.

4. Brené Brown, *The Gifts of Imperfection: Let Go of Who You Think You're Supposed to Be and Embrace Who You Are* (Center City, MN: Hazelden, 2010), 63.

5. Phillips Brooks, quoted in E. Carver McGriff, *Lectionary Preaching Workbook, series VI, cycle C* (Lima, OH: CSS Publishing, 2000), 176.

CHAPTER SEVEN

1. Electronic newsletter from David to his staff, July 2015. Used by permission.

2. Electronic newsletter from David to his staff, July 2015. Used by permission.

3. Duane Elmer, *Cross-Cultural Servanthood: Serving the World in Christlike Humility* (Downers Grove, IL: InterVarsity, 2006), 156.

4. Robert K. Greenleaf, "The Servant as Leader" (1970), quoted in "What Is Servant Leadership?", Robert K. Greenleaf Center for Servant Leadership, www.greenleaf.org/what-is-servant-leadership/; emphasis added.

5. Buck Owens, "Act Naturally," *All-Time Greatest Hits* © 2010 Saguaro Road Records.

6. Michelle, quoted in "69: Learn to Lead: Ten Skills Every New Leader Must Master: Servant Attitude," HansFinzel.com, October 9, 2015, www.hansfinzel.com/69; emphasis added.

7. "BP CEO: 'I'd Like My Life Back,'" ABC News video, 0:23, December 29, 2010, http://abcnews.go.com/GMA/video/bp-ceo-tony-hayward-i-would-like-my-life-back-12503979.

8. "BP Chief: 'We Care About the Small People,'" YouTube video, 0:55, posted by Associated Press, June 16, 2010, www.youtube.com/watch?v=th3LtLx0IEM.

9. Timothy Laniak, *While Shepherds Watch Their Flocks: Forty Daily Reflections on Biblical Leadership* (ShepherdLeader Publications, 2007), 29.

10. Zig Ziglar, *See You at the Top* (Gretna, LA: Pelican, 2000), 45.

11. Jim Collins, "Level 5 Leadership," chap. 2 in *Good to Great: Why Some Companies Make the Leap ... and Others Don't* (New York: HarperCollins, 2001).

CHAPTER EIGHT

1. "Management Tip of the Day: Don't Forsake Managing for Leading," *Reuters*, November 11, 2010, www.reuters.com/article/us-management-tip-thursday-idUSTRE6AA2X720101111.

2. Lou Cannon, *President Reagan: The Role of a Lifetime* (New York: PublicAffairs, 2000), 154.

3. John Ortberg, "John Ortberg on Hope Management," *Christianity Today*, February 2008, www.christianitytoday.com/pastors/2008/february-on line-only/cln80211.html.

4. Brené Brown, *The Gifts of Imperfection: Let Go of Who You Think You're Supposed to Be and Embrace Who You Are* (Center City, MN: Hazelden, 2010), 56.

CHAPTER NINE

1. William J. Broad, "Toppling Theories, Scientists Find 6 Slits, Not Big Gash, Sank Titanic," *New York Times*, April 8, 1997, www.nytimes. com/1997/04/08/science/toppling-theories-scientists-find-6-slits-not-big -gash-sank-titanic.html?pagewanted=all.

2. Guilbert Gates et al., "Explaining Volkswagen's Emissions Scandal," *New York Times*, September 12, 2016, www.nytimes.com/interactive/2015/business /international/vw-diesel-emissions-scandal-explained.html?_r=0.

3. Jordan Robertson and Rachel Metz, "Hurd Gets $28 Million Package to Leave HP," *SFGate*, August 8, 2010, www.sfgate.com/business/article /Hurd-gets-28-million-package-to-leave-HP-3178914.php.

4. Bette Midler, "From a Distance," *Some People's Lives* © 2005 Atlantic Recording.

5. Ethel Waters, "His Eye Is on the Sparrow," *His Eye Is on the Sparrow* © 2014 Photoplay Records.

6. John Wooden, quoted in Pat Williams, *Coach Wooden's Greatest Secret: The Power of a Lot of Little Things Done Well* (Grand Rapids, MI: Revell, 2014), 140.

7. Warren Bennis and Burt Nanus, *Leaders: Strategies for Taking Charge*, 2nd ed. (New York: HarperCollins, 2003), xii.

8. John C. Maxwell, email message to author, September 2007. Used by permission.

9. Robert Clinton, "Leadership Emergence Patterns" (lectures, Fuller Seminary, Pasadena, CA, 1987–1989).

CHAPTER TEN

1. Dwight L. Moody, quoted in Charles R. Swindoll, *Moses: A Man of Selfless Dedication* (Nashville: Thomas Nelson, 1999), 20.

2. "'You've Got to Find What You Love,' Jobs Says," Stanford University, June 14, 2005, http://news.stanford.edu/2005/06/14/jobs-061505/.

3. Howard Hendricks, quoted in Zig Ziglar, *Better Than Good: Creating a Life You Can't Wait to Live* (Nashville: Thomas Nelson, 2006), 179.

4. Jim Collins, "Level 5 Leadership," chap. 2 in *Good to Great: Why Some Companies Make the Leap ... And Others Don't* (New York: HarperCollins, 2001).

5. Fyodor Dostoevsky, *The Brothers Karamazov: A Novel in Four Parts and an Epilogue*, trans. David McDuff (New York: Penguin, 2003), 413.

RECOMMENDED READING

Arbinger Institute. *Leadership and Self-Deception: Getting out of the Box.* San Francisco: Berrett-Koehler, 2010.

Bradberry, Travis, and Jean Greaves. *Emotional Intelligence 2.0.* San Diego: TalentSmart, 2009.

Brown, Brené. *Daring Greatly: How the Courage to Be Vulnerable Transforms the Way We Live, Love, Parent, and Lead.* New York: Avery, 2015.

Clinton, Robert. *The Making of a Leader: Recognizing the Lessons and Stages of Leadership Development.* Rev. ed. Colorado Springs: NavPress, 2012.

Cloud, Henry, and John Townsend. *Boundaries: When to Say Yes, How to Say No to Take Control of Your Life.* Grand Rapids, MI: Zondervan, 1992.

Cloud, Henry. *Necessary Endings: The Employees, Businesses, and Relationships That All of Us Have to Give Up in Order to Move Forward.* New York: HarperCollins, 2010.

De Mello, Anthony. *Awareness: The Perils and Opportunities of Reality.* New York: Image Books, 1990.

Goleman, Daniel, Annie McKee, and Richard E. Boyatzis. *Primal Leadership: Unleashing the Power of Emotional Intelligence.* Boston: Harvard Business, 2013.

Hersey, Paul. *The Situational Leader. 4th ed.* Cary, NC: Center for Leadership Studies, 1992.

Kegan, Robert, and Lisa Laskow Lahey. *Immunity to Change: How to Overcome It and Unlock the Potential in Yourself and Your Organization.* Boston: Harvard Business, 2009.

Loehr, Jim, and Tony Schwartz. *The Power of Full Engagement: Managing Energy, Not Time, Is the Key to High Performance and Personal Renewal.* New York: Free Press, 2003.

Shaw, Haydn. *Sticking Points: How to Get 4 Generations Working Together in the 12 Places They Come Apart.* Carol Stream, IL: Tyndale, 2013.

ABOUT THE AUTHOR

Dr. Hans Finzel is a successful leader, author, speaker, and trusted authority in the field of leadership. For twenty years, he served as president of international nonprofit WorldVenture. Today, he serves as president of HDLeaders, and he teaches and speaks globally on all things leadership. Hans speaks, writes, and teaches on practical leadership principles from the real world—not just the classroom. He has written ten books, including his bestseller, *The Top Ten Mistakes Leaders Make*, and *The Top Ten Leadership Commandments*. Hans has trained leaders on five

continents, and his books have been translated into over twenty
foreign languages.

Connect with Hans:
>   Website: hansfinzel.com
>   Twitter: @hansfinzel
>   Facebook: facebook.com/hansfinzel
>   YouTube: youtube.com/hansfinzel

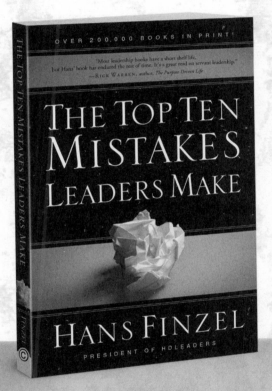

Based on the life and legacy of Moses, these ten scriptural principles can **revolutionize** **your business, your ministry, even your life.**

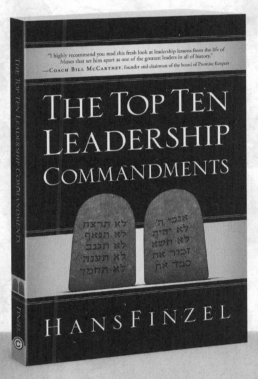

The life of Moses provides an example of what it means to be an effective leader. Consider his pedigree: he answered the call to do something beyond his means; he stood his ground before kings; he led millions of people on a journey across rivers and through deserts. Moses did all of this with a dogged persistence. In *The Top Ten Leadership Commandments*, you will discover a dynamic, effective tool for developing leadership skills, all built on the solid foundation of God's Word.